Elena Lucrezia

Cornaro Piscopia

1646-1684

A grant

from The Hunt Foundation

to the University of Pittsburgh

has made possible

the publication of this commemorative volume

ELENA LUCREZIA CORNARO PISCOPIA

1646-1684

(*Panel opposite page:* Translation from Latin)
Think not this is a portrait of Minerva.
You have the name inscribed; none the less you will
Be as many-eyed as Argus.

Helena Lucretia Cornaro Piscopia, laurel-endowed in Philosophy at Padua, in the year 1678, June 25, by Carolo Renaldo, Philosopher and first-ranking Professor.

Jacobus Franciscus Cassionus, *Sculptor*

Museo Civico Padua

Quam cernis pictam ne credas esse Mineruam
Scriptum nomen habes, attamen argus eris
Helena Lucretia Cornelia Piscopia ad Phil: laur: promota
Pat. Ann: 1678 Die 25 Iunij a Carolo Renaldino Philo:
soph: è prima sede profitente.

Ia: Fran: Cassonus sculp:

Elena Lucrezia Cornaro Piscopia 1646–1684.
Prima Donna Laureata nel Mondo.

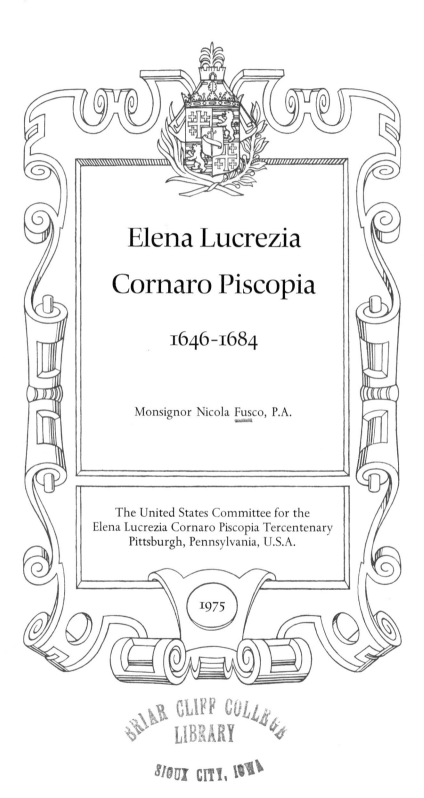

Elena Lucrezia
Cornaro Piscopia

1646-1684

Monsignor Nicola Fusco, P.A.

The United States Committee for the
Elena Lucrezia Cornaro Piscopia Tercentenary
Pittsburgh, Pennsylvania, U.S.A.

1975

In loving memory
the four sons of
Rachel McMasters Miller Hunt
and Roy Arthur Hunt
dedicate this book
to their mother
and to
Monsignor Nicola Fusco
author, bibliophile, builder, man of God
whose victories Rachel Hunt encouraged
whose scholarly interests she shared
and whose friendship she valued.

Table of Contents

List of Illustrations

Foreword

ALMOST forty years ago, in the Alcoa office of my father, Roy Arthur Hunt, I first met the late Monsignor Nicola Fusco of New Kensington, Pennsylvania. At the time, the mid-1930s, my father was President of Aluminum Company of America, which had a large fabricating plant there. Father Fusco, who later became The Right Reverend Monsignor Fusco, Prothonotary Apostolic, was pastor of the largest of the city's three Roman Catholic churches and spiritual leader of the substantial Italian community.

It was impossible to be his neighbor, as Alcoa was, without becoming deeply interested in Father Fusco, as steadfastly he went about organizing his people and his many friends in the community to build beautiful Mount Saint Peter and its complex of church, parish house, convent, and school. He was, throughout the years, until his tragic death in 1971, a cherished friend of the Hunt family.

Dad, though a staunch Episcopalian, respected Father Fusco's ability to inspire in his people the desire to furnish, as a labor-of-love, the material and the financial resources, from inside and outside his parish, to translate Mount Saint Peter into a church of great aesthetic and spiritual beauty. He respected, too, Father Fusco's understanding of the importance of Alcoa in the lives of many of his people who worked in the Allegheny Valley.

Mother's interest in and love for books and for the work of

scholars and craftsmen who wrote and bound books were warmly understood and appreciated by Father Fusco. The Monsignor and Mother spent many charmed hours, both in his library at Mount Saint Peter and in her library at our home, sharing mutual enthusiasms.

I remember one evening at dinner when Mother discussed with the Monsignor her dream to keep together permanently her collection of botanical books and incunabula in a new library, which, of course, the Monsignor encouraged Dad to provide.

Today, the Hunt Botanical Library at Carnegie-Mellon University houses, in a setting of appropriate beauty and suitability for scholars and bibliophiles, Mother's collection of books and prints. A tribute paid her by Dr. George H. M. Lawrence, former Director of the Library, may perhaps illustrate why my brothers and I wish her to share with the Monsignor the dedication of this book:

"Rachel Hunt was very much a humanist who revered books not as items solely of beauty, of utility, or of great intrinsic value, but also as the products of the intellect and hands of persons, who as creative individuals left something of themselves in works that lived after them. From this, it was only natural that she was ever ready to share her interest and knowledge, and to give encouragement to anyone she met who likewise was a lover of books. Her early recognition of kindred feelings on the part of Father Fusco without doubt contributed materially to the mutual respect and admiration held by each for the other."

And so, this Foreword introduces a book honoring our family's long friendship with its author, a book which my brothers, Tod, Roy and Rick, and I believe Mother and Dad would be pleased with as a fitting contribution to the Tercentenary of a day in June 1678 when, from the venerable University of Padua, Elena Lucrezia Cornaro Piscopia, first woman laureate in the world, received the degree *Magistra et Doctrix Philosophiae.*

We also wish to record here our admiration for Father Francis L. Ginocchi, who succeeded Monsignor Fusco at Mount Saint Peter and who is faithfully following his preceptor's tradition.

ALFRED M. HUNT

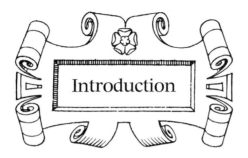

Introduction

THIS book holds meaning for many people. Its heart is a gentle life story of Elena Lucrezia Cornaro Piscopia, the first woman ever to receive a university degree, as her life unfolded for the author, Nicola Fusco, more than 250 years after her death in Padua, city of her Alma Mater. The *Dedication*, the *Foreword*, and this *Introduction* accent the more personal meanings. The comprehensive *Bibliography* by Dr. Maria Tonzig will mean much to scholars penetrating the Baroque era in which Elena Cornaro lived. American women who have worked for years to open doors of opportunity to women should experience a very real sense of satisfaction when they find this book listed in library card catalogues.

My *Introduction* reflects an endeavor of many years to unravel and reweave the threads of destiny that have carried the story of Elena Lucrezia Cornaro Piscopia from the Old World westward across the Atlantic. This is a twentieth-century story.

At the turn of the century, through the gift of an American woman, Elena Lucrezia Cornaro Piscopia became part of the tradition of one of the first American women's colleges. In the middle of the century, Cornaro became part of the daily life of the first university west of the Alleghenies. Finally, in the third quarter, a gift in honor of an American woman, whose collection of botanical books is recognized as of first importance, brought reality to the dreams of a group of Pittsburgh women representing colleges, universities, and two world-wide women's organizations. These women had long been working on plans to celebrate the 300th anniversary in 1978 of the first granting to a woman the degree *Magistra et Doctrix Philosophiae*. As a result, this book, with its valuable contribution to the Cornaro story written by an imaginative churchman of Italian heritage, will be presented to libraries of colleges and universities and to collections of books about women in time to provide source material for 1978 ceremonies paying tribute to Elena Lucrezia Cornaro Piscopia throughout the world.

Nicola Fusco—Scholar, Author, Bibliophile, and Priest

Nicola Fusco was born in 1887 in Formicola, a small Italian town between Rome and Naples. His forebears were of ancient and highly respected Roman stock. Because of political and economic changes in Italy, Nicola's father, a younger son, emigrated in 1891 to the United States—with his wife, his five daughters, and a very young son. Nicola, his older son, he left in Italy, under the guardianship of Nicola's uncle, Don Giuseppe Fusco, archpriest of Formicola, to continue education in the Minor Seminary of Caiazzo.

After the death of his uncle, in 1906, Nicola joined his family in Pittsburgh, Pennsylvania and continued his religious studies. In 1912 he graduated from Saint Vincent College, at the Benedictine Archabbey near Latrobe, Pennsylvania. There he read widely in a library rich in classical studies, and began his writing and his collecting of books for a library of his own. To his writing style in his new tongue, English, he added the charm of his native Italian expression.

His first parish was Saint Lawrence Church in Hillsville, a stone quarry hamlet in Lawrence County, Pennsylvania. In the solitude of its rolling hills (so noted Dr. F. J. Pessolano of New Kensington, Pennsylvania) "history and literature became part of the Man." Among the Italian, Polish, and Slovene parishioners, Father Fusco began a generous life of counseling, inspiring, and guiding immigrants, lonely in a strange land.

In 1923 Father Fusco became pastor of Saint Peter's Church in New Kensington, a small wooden church with a membership of only two hundred Italian families, in a population of ten thousand Italian-Americans.

Father Fusco began what he called "A Crusade of Repossession" among these people, too many of whom were alienated from the Church and not adjusted to life in a new country. They ignored the young pastor of the little church. But Father was determined. He attended meetings in the Italian clubs. He visited families, door to door. Soon the warmth of his personality and his helpfulness in solving their problems brought rewards. The little church was filled to capacity every Sunday, and those who came late stood or knelt on the steps, outside.

Parish work and supervision of mission assignments in adjacent communities multiplied Father Fusco's spiritual demands. He sought refuge as often as he could in the study which housed his collection of old and rare books. At this desk, among his books, shelved from floor to ceiling, he meditated and wrote essays in history and biography. He had published a book of verse in Italy. His first work published in New Kensington was a series of memories of his old home in Formicola. He also contributed editorials to three Italian religious periodicals. Throughout his life he continued to publish much of humane scholarship. He said his writing and his library refreshed him to turn, with energy renewed, to the needs of his parish and its people.

In 1936 Father Fusco led a pilgrimage to Italy. And it was on this trip that he discovered Elena Lucrezia Cornaro Piscopia, affectionately called "the Cornaro." Of that discovery he tells in the first chapter of this book, so I need not repeat.

When back in New Kensington, Father Fusco began and completed the most ambitious undertaking of his life—the building of a new larger and more substantial church. Five acres of ground on a hill nearby were purchased in 1939. In 1940, the heirs of a distinguished Pittsburgher decided to raze their family home and give the sloping lawns with their great trees and gardens to the City of Pittsburgh for a park. A member of Father Fusco's parish, John Stanish, knew the stately mansion well. He thought that the materials, both exterior and interior, might be used for the new church. Together they visited the vacant house awaiting the swinging ball of a wrecking company.

Father Fusco's imagination caught fire. Hours of dreaming and of prayer were translated into an agreement whereby the red Michigan sandstone of the exterior and the marble, woodwork, and wrought iron of the interior would be removed to the New Kensington hilltop by members of Saint Peter's parish for the construction of the new church—all under the direction of Monsignor's close friend John Stanish. Ground was broken for the new church in 1940. In 1944, despite the shortage in materials and manpower of World War II, the complex of church, parish house, parochial school, and convent was completed. The story of that great accomplishment is told in detail in Father Fusco's dedication book entitled, "Mount Saint Peter."

In the 1950s Father Nicola Fusco won signal honors for both his distinguished writings and his service to the church: from the Republic of Italy, the *Commendatore;* from Saint Vincent College, the honorary *Doctor of Laws;* from the Papacy, the right to be called *Monsignore.* In 1961 Pope John XXIII called him to Rome as a *Consultor* in the Commission for Discipline of the Clergy and the Christian Laity. And in 1966 he was appointed by Pope Paul VI an honorary *Prothonotary Apostolic,* which invests the one honored with the status of a bishop without a diocese.

[8]

The Italian Classroom, University of Pittsburgh
The Cornaro Window, Vassar College
The Cornaro Grave, Padua

My association with Monsignor Fusco came about in connection with my work at the University of Pittsburgh where I had developed an international program, Cultural and Educational Exchange, for faculties and students. This program grew naturally out of my earlier work of many years organizing Nationality Committees to help the University establish a series of classrooms representing the cultural heritage of nationality groups which have enriched life in Pittsburgh.

The Italians began plans for their beautiful Renaissance Room in the Cathedral of Learning as far back as 1927. I told a group of Italian women about the stained glass window in the library at Vassar College, first American women's college to recognize the first woman in the world to graduate from a university—the young Venetian, Elena Lucrezia Cornaro Piscopia, who received the Doctor of Philosophy degree from the University of Padua on June 25, 1678. The Italian women decided, then and there, that there must be a painting of her in the Italian classroom. It was not until after World War II that a famous Italian painter of women, Giovanni Romagnoli of Bologna, was invited to come to Pittsburgh and paint a mural of the Cornaro above the walnut panelling on the rear wall of the Italian Classroom.

Monsignor Fusco had long been a friend of Romagnoli. He went at once to see his friend at work in the Italian Classroom. There he discovered that the theme was Elena Lucrezia Cornaro Piscopia, whose statue at the University of Padua had excited his interest and curiosity in 1936. The Monsignor made up his mind to see what more he could find out about this learned young woman in Saint Vincent's libraries and in Rome. The fruits of his research appeared in an article entitled

THE GREAT WINDOW, Vassar College Thompson Memorial Library. Elena Piscopia (center) defending her thesis before scholar-examinant and public audience in the Cathedral of Padua. [*Glossary* p 96]

[10]

MURAL, Italian Classroom, University of Pittsburgh. Elena Piscopia surrounded by symbols of her learning.

Inscription on wall of Italian Room
Left of Mural: Helena Lucretia e gente Patricia Cornaro-Piscopia Venetiis orta prima quae inter foeminas omnes philosophiae lauream in Patavina Universitate consequi meruit.   MDCLXXVIII
Translation: Helena Lucretia Cornaro Piscopia, born in Venice of patrician lineage, first woman of all time to attain the laureate in philosophy—from the University of Padua, 1678.
Right of Mural: Italiae feminea proles eiusque sodales, eandem Italiam litterarum, artium, iurisque magistram grato animo recolentes, fecerunt hoc opus fieri.   MDCCCCXLIX
Translation: Women of Italian lineage, bound to the motherland in common social bond, cherishing, as due, with grateful hearts this Italian teacher of literature, arts, and law, have had this masterpiece made. 1949.
Giovanni Romagnoli, *Artist*

Photograph by Thomas C. Pears III

"Elena Lucrezia Cornaro Piscopia—1646-1684," published in the May 1949 issue of *Lucerna,* an Italian cultural magazine printed by the Columbia University Press. The article was illustrated with a reproduction of the Romagnoli mural and a photograph of the artist himself in the Italian Classroom. A copy of this issue was sent to the University of Pittsburgh and placed in the files of the Italian Classroom Committee. There it rested for twenty years, 1949-1969.

During these years the Cultural Exchange Program at the University grew steadily. Eighteen Nationality Committees, their classrooms finished, started a new program of scholarship awards to enable University of Pittsburgh students to go abroad for summer study in Italy. All students who went to Italy were encouraged to visit Padua and the grave of the Cornaro in the Romanesque-Gothic Chapel of Saint Luke in the present Renaissance Basilica of Saint Justina. The entire mortuary chapel, long unused and neglected, needs restoration. By 1895 the Cornaro gravestone had disintegrated and with its original Latin inscription was replaced. This 1895 gravestone has now been fragmented and must be replaced.

Editor's Note: In the *Glossary* are data relative to the Vassar Library stained glass window, to the Saint Luke Chapel, and to the gravesite—information gathered since Monsignor's *Profile* was written.

The Cornaro Manuscript and the Death of Monsignor Nicola Fusco, P.A.

In the autumn of 1969, I received a letter from the newly installed abbot of Saint Justina, Don Innocenzo de Angelis, who had learned of my interest in the Cornaro through cor-

Marble statue of Elena Piscopia (The Cornaro), University of Padua, viewed by University of Pittsburgh students, 1952.

Foto Lux Padova

[13]

Pittsburgh students *(Quo Vadis)* lay flowers on the second Cornaro gravestone given in 1895 by Abbess Matilda Pynsent of Benedictine Monastery, Rome.

Dr. Tonzig, Dr. Mitchell, Father Ruperto Pepi (Historian, Saint Justina Benedictine Community) watch Don Pio Miotto trying to assemble the fragmented Cornaro gravestone, which the Abbess Matilda Pynsent and other dignitaries had placed on the grave in 1895.

Foto Cine Piran Padova

Doctor Maria Tonzig (Padua), Doctor Ruth Crawford Mitchell (Pittsburgh) at The Cornaro's coffin, 1969, which was disinterred in 1968 when plans were being considered for a Gothic restoration of the Saint Luke Chapel.

respondence filed by his predecessor. He suggested I come to Padua to see the Chapel and discuss what might be done to restore the gravesite in time for the observation of the 1978 Tercentenary of Elena Cornaro's graduation. The invitation was a challenge to an American woman whose undergraduate years had been spent at Vassar College with its magnificent Cornaro Window, and whose academic working years had been spent at the University of Pittsburgh with its Cornaro mural.

When I returned from my visit to Padua I went through the old Italian Committee files and found Monsignor's *Lucerna* article. I took steps immediately to meet Monsignor Fusco. Together the Monsignor and I examined the mass of material I had brought back from Padua. He was sympathetic to the idea of making his article into a book to help celebrate the Tercentenary of 1978—there being almost no information in English in university and college libraries about this first woman in the world to be awarded the Doctor of Philosophy degree.

One evening in early November 1971, John Stanish, the Monsignor's devoted friend and secretary, telephoned me to say, "Monsignor wishes you to have, *this very night,* the Cornaro life, revised for the third time. . . . He wants to be ready." John delivered the manuscript to me with his own hands.

Two days later, November 3, 1971, Monsignor Nicola Fusco and John Stanish were both killed in an automobile accident on William Penn Highway near Latrobe, returning from confession at Saint Vincent College Chapel.

An editorial tribute in the *Pittsburgh Post-Gazette,* headlined *"Last of the Missionary Priests,"* noted "from the period of the great Italian immigration to Western Pennsylvania, he was not only priest, but social worker, advisor, often judge among his people." And of his devotion to ecumenism, a leading Presbyterian pastor wrote: "Once in a while God gives a gift of a life that is more public than private—a man (or woman) who is the sum total of a thousand different heartbeats. Nicola Fusco was one man. But as one man, he was everyman."

Today there are many lasting memorials to Nicola Fusco, in buildings, in books—this book—and in the hearts and minds of men and women—memorials to the aesthetic sensitivity and romantic imagination which nourished the disciplined life of this man of God.

RUTH CRAWFORD MITCHELL

A Profile

First Acquaintance

DURING the summer of 1936, I happened to be in Padua, City of the Domes, the birthplace of Livy, Valerius Flaccus, Ascanius Pedianus, Thrasea Paetus, Squarcione, Emperor Henry IV, Andrea Mantegna, Luigi Cornaro, and many others of world-wide fame. No longer is the city the "rich House of Merchants," as it was called by Andre Maurel, but still the glory of past splendor is in evidence everywhere.

Here one walks upon the same cobblestones which Dante Alighieri and Petrach once trod in their quest for peace. Here the life and light which Giotto, Sansovino, Bellini, Donatello, and Michelangelo left behind surround one incessantly, constant as the roar of the ocean in a shell, and indelible as the image of God on the soul of man.

After a visit to the magnificent basilica of St. Anthony, the *Doctor Evangelicus* of the universal Church who filled this city and the world with his wonders, I went to the renowned University of Padua which was founded in 1222 under the name *Studium Patavinum*. Through the long centuries since then it has contributed generously to the civilization and progress of the world.

Here, among the many names of teachers or alumni we find the name Galileo Galilei (1564-1641). He taught mathematics and astronomy, and while teaching at the University invented the first complete astronomical telescope which enabled him to make a series of memorable discoveries about

[21]

the Moon, Jupiter, Venus, and the Sun. Finally he proved that the Earth does revolve around the Sun, so that he stood firm before the Inquisition with his famous phrase "E pur si muove." (But it does move!)

In the seventeenth century, after more than four hundred years of intellectual and scientific revelations, the University of Padua still was recognized in the world of learning as a great source of light which pushed the sap of life through the veins of all those hungry for knowledge—a magnificent intellectual center open to men of all nations.

Scattered through the broad halls and spacious rooms are inscriptions, tablets, and tall statues which honor Cardinal Bembo (1470-1549), Sperone Speroni (1500-1588), Albertus Magnus (1193-1280), Vesalius (1533-1564), Acquapendente (1533-1619), Pomponazzi (1462-1525), the English Cardinal Reginald Pole (1500-1558), Scaliger (1484-1558), Torquato Tasso (1544-1595), Sobieski (1624-1693), and many more great men who were involved in the life of the University.

At the foot of the stairway leading to the second floor gallery of the old University building stands a marble statue of a young woman, in appearance like the ancient concept of a goddess. Her features have an intellectual beauty which could have moved Shelley to sing:

> Spirit of beauty, that dost consecrate
> With thine own hues all thou dost shine upon
> Of human thought or form—Where art thou gone?
> Why dost thou pass away and leave our state,
> This dim vale of tears, vacant and desolate?

On the pedestal a long Latin inscription tells us that the statue represents Elena Lucrezia Cornaro Piscopia who lived during the second half of the seventeenth century.

The Illustrious House of Cornaro

ELENA LUCREZIA CORNARO PISCOPIA! Who was she? Why does she deserve a statue among all these famous men in this celebrated place of learning? I made some inquiries, but when I left it I knew no more about the lady, distinguished though she might have been in her day, than I did when I came to Padua. And for a long time I did not think of her again.

However, in 1949, in Pittsburgh, Pennsylvania, I met a dear friend, Giovanni Romagnoli of Bologna, internationally acclaimed as one of the great Italian portrait painters of his time.

"Well, what are you doing in Pittsburgh?" I asked him.

"I am painting the Piscopia woman in the Italian Classroom of the Cathedral of Learning. The portrait is almost finished. Do you want to see it?"

So once again I met Elena Lucrezia Cornaro Piscopia. What Romagnoli told me about this heroine excited me. She was, I found, not only as beautiful as any of Bronzino's Madonnas, but could easily claim all the virtues listed in the Vatican Stanzas of Raphael, and I immediately sought all available information on Elena Piscopia.

The New York Public Library and the Carnegie Library of Pittsburgh had very little about her. In the rich monastic library of the Benedictine Archabbey of Saint Vincent, Latrobe, Pennsylvania, I found the material I needed to begin my study.

The Venetian House of the Cornaro was ennobled and

famous not only because a long-lived legend traced its lineage back to the Roman family of the Cornelii, but because, during the thirteenth and seventeenth centuries, it gave four doges to the Venetian Republic, three popes and eight cardinals to the Church, many great statesmen to Italy, and a queen to the Island of Cyprus.

Caterina Cornaro was the queen. Titian, Tintoretto, and Paulo Veronese have shown us her opulent beauty. But today, art and history reveal her more perceptively, and we learn that her intellectual attainments by far surpassed her physical beauty.

While her husband, King James of Lusignan, was at war with Greece to defend his sovereignty over Cyprus, Armenia, and Jerusalem, Caterina obtained a very large loan from her uncle, Federigo Cornaro of San Luca. In recognition of this service, King James conferred upon Federigo and his heirs the title "Knights of Cyprus" and made them lords of a castle called "Piscopia."

Thus, one of the branches of the Cornaros added Piscopia to its already illustrious name. A descendant of this family was Gianbattista Cornaro Piscopia, the father of Elena Lucrezia Cornaro Piscopia. She was born in Venice June 5, 1646.

The Family Background

IN his youth, Gianbattista was what today we might call a playboy. Youth that does not use wealth foolishly when it is at hand, is a rarity in any age. In later years, however, he made ample amends for youthful excesses and follies by becoming an exemplary father and citizen, wholly devoted to the education of his children and to the service of the Venetian Republic.

In his old age he is described in public documents as "Uomo di gran spirito e testa, et singulare abilitate, et come tale da tutti considerato." (A man of great spirit and mind, of singular intelligence, and considered such by all who knew him.)

In the meantime, however, after he had sown his wild oats, he married a woman who was neither his equal, nor his ideal. "The reason for such matrimony is patrimony," says Ogden Nash.

In his turbulent youth, Gianbattista had had no time to think about preserving his vast inheritance and the woman he married did not think about anything else. Her name was Zanetta Giovanna Boni; but she was nicknamed Valdesabia, probably because she was a native of Val di Sabia, a town near the city of Novara in the Piedmont. She bore him five children: Francesco, Girolamo, Caterina, Elena Lucrezia, and another Caterina (the first Caterina died at an early age).

Francesco died without leaving children. Girolamo begat two daughters, Elena and Lucrezia, undoubtedly both names

Elena Cornaro Piscopia, Age 22
(See facing page for translation)

Translation of Latin (frame)

Helena Cornelia Piscopia, her age 22, daughter of Giovanni Baptista, chief administrator, San Marco.

Jean Langlois, *Sculptor*

Translation of Latin Elegiac Couplets

There are twin Helens: one Holy, and the other
lovely. A third in character and beauty both resemble.

Another

Helen is committed to the Cross: You are committed to
the Glory of Christianity,
O Helen. The Cross yields to Her, and She to you.

Signed: Brother Franciscus Macedo, from Saint Augustine

[Editor's Note: *Her* and *She* refer to the Church, the
Glory of Christianity]

The Same in Metrical Greek

There are two Helens, one holy, the other very lovely.
You resemble the third in character and form.

Another

For Helen there is the Cross, for you the Glory of
Christ,
O Helen. The Cross yields to Her, the Glory of
Christ to you.

Signed: Gradenici Archpriest: a Greek, her teacher

Museo Civico

given in honor of his sister, their celebrated aunt. With these brothers, Francesco and Girolamo, the male branch of the Cornaro Piscopia family came to an end. The second Caterina married one of the Vendramins; her virtues and talents attracted no little attention both in Italy and abroad. However, the name Cornaro Piscopia did not drop into oblivion with the end of the male line: our Elena Lucrezia has made it immortal.

Elena's father, Gianbattista, during her early years provided the secure background of an established Venetian family. He was the Procurator of San Marco, an office which he administered with dignity. He gained much respect throughout Italy, because he kept the office remarkably free from political intrigue. He was lodged, according to records in the archives of the Venetian Republic, in the Palace in Piazza San Marco. "He was charged to hold three audiences weekly, and was not allowed, without permission from the Great Council, to be absent more than two days a month. His chief duties were to superintend the Cathedral, the treasury of Saint Marc, to take legal guardianship of the orphans, and to be the public executor to such as chose to appoint him."

Honorable as the post was in the Venice of the 1600s, it was won, as was the custom then, by what today we call open purchase. When Gianbattista, in 1649, applied for the coveted office, he gave 25,000 ducats to the public treasury. Elena Lucrezia was then three years old. Ten years later, after her father had apparently been out of office for some time, he found it harder—and more expensive—to get himself and his children back into the famous *Libro d'Oro* of the Republic, the Who's Who of Venice. His unhappy marriage proved the main obstacle, for his wife enjoyed neither a good family background nor a good personal reputation.

His offer of 40,000 ducats was rejected; then, some years later, another of 100,000 ducats met an equal fate. But Gianbattista persisted, and on March 1, 1664, when Elena Lucrezia was eight-

[28]

een, the Great Council accepted him as Procurator, with 693 yeas, 286 nays, and 47 abstentions (ducats unknown). Well might the Venetian Archives note "Era Procurator per soldi." (He bought the office.) Yet, according to the same records, Gianbattista was greatly respected for his conduct of the post which officials of the declining Venice, financially drained by the Turkish wars (1645-1668), held at so high a selling price.

Education in Venice

MEANWHILE, as her father desperately tried to better the family fortunes securing titles and honors, his daughter worked to immortalize it by her learning.

"Ego studii," she wrote, about 1672, to her father from Padua, "laetitia, aeris salubritate, atque diligenti cura medicorum satis viribus utor, quare in spem sum in posterum posse me navare operam studiis et Domus nostrae nomen ab interitu vindicare." (With the joy of my studies, the salubrity of the air, and the diligent care of the physicians, I feel much stronger; therefore, I hope that in the future I may resume my studies and thus rescue the name of our House from extinction and oblivion.)

It should be noted that this excerpt from the young girl's letter shows, first, that her health was the cause of some concern, and that to her and, presumably, to others of the Venetian hierarchy, scholarship was a mark of distinction not only for temporary reward but for lasting fame.

The parish priest of Saint Luke's Congregation in Venice had discovered that Elena Lucrezia was truly an infant prodigy. At seven she had exhibited marvelous reasoning powers, an astonishing memory, and a noble soul. At the insistence of Monsignor Gianbattista Fabris, she was tutored by John Valier, Doctor Bartolotti, Alexander Anderson, and Luigi Ambrosio Grandenigo in grammar, music, Latin, and Greek. Later, a Jesuit, whose name has since been lost, taught her mathematics.

At seventeen she was an expert musician and a charming soprano. She played, with delicate mastery, the harpsichord, the clavichord, the harp, the violin; she also composed music.

At this time, Carlo Rinardini, celebrated professor at the University of Pisa and later at the Studium of Padua, met the young lady and wrote: "She is as beautiful as an angel and speaks Greek, Latin, French, English, and Spanish, with perfect ease."

As an aid to her theological studies—which she preferred to all others—she learned Hebrew under the rabbi of the Venetian Synagogue, as well as Arabic and Chaldaic under other professors whose names have not been recorded. Rinardini also reported that she conversed about theology, philosophy, dialectics, mathematics, and astronomy "with no mediocre acumen."

Indeed, the most learned professors of her day, Giacomo Fiorelli, Giovanni Palazzi, Francesco Macedo, Carlo Patino, Fulvio Frugoni, Gianbattista Vitali, Giacomo Zopelli, Gianbattista Pacchinelli, Gian Lorenzo Lucchesini, Giorgio Calafatti, Christopher Ivanovich, spared no words to express their awed admiration of her.

Today many who go to Rome pay their respect to the Pope; so in her day great men who visited Padua called on Elena Lucrezia Cornaro Piscopia. Gianbattista Cornaro Piscopia was himself no longer honored and privileged simply because he was the Procurator of San Marco or a member of an illustrious and very wealthy Venetian family. He was respected because he was the father of the phenomenal maiden who had mastered the "sciblis" of her time—which means she had mastered almost the entire body of knowledge gathered by ancient, medieval, and seventeenth century scholars.

Henry Houtinger, in 1665, dedicated his *Historia Ecclesiastica Saeculi XIV* "to the father of a very great daughter."

The famous Swiss writer, Madame Louise Frotte de Windsor,

rebuked Gregorio Leti for not mentioning Elena Lucrezia in his monumental work *Italia Regnante,* published in Valencia during the year 1675. "Une Dame de qui le mérite seul donne du prix a tout le sexe et au réparer tous les défauts." (It is unpardonable to omit the name "of a Lady whose merits honor her sex and redeem it of all its defects.") Leti published a second edition of his work in 1676 and devoted thirty-nine pages of the fourth volume to Elena Cornaro.

Scientists, bishops, cardinals, and princes from many countries came to the great Palazzo Cornaro in Venice, and later to the smaller Palazzo Cornaro at Padua, to have the privilege of seeing and hearing the prodigious lady. The academic *Disputationes* in which she took part were great events. To be invited to them was an honor, and to attend them was a memorable experience.

Pope Innocent XI and King John III of Poland, who could not come to hear her, instead, sent letters praising her virtues and learning.

Illustrations on facing page

Top: Oldest building, University of Padua, where Elena Piscopia attended classes, 1672-1678. Still used today (20th Century).

Bottom: Two floors of galleries with colonnades surrounding inner courtyard. Coats of Arms of famous faculty and graduates are on walls and ceiling, first floor. The marble statue of The Cornaro is at the foot of the stairs leading to the second floor gallery. These etchings are reproduced from *L'Università di Padova* by Antonio Favaro. Venice OFF Grafiche C. Ferrari 1922.

Studies at the University of Padua

IN 1672 Elena Lucrezia moved from the Palazzo Cornaro in the parish of San Luca in Venice to the Palazzo Cornaro in Padua, to continue her studies nearer to the University of Padua. In those days, Padua was among the most famous centers of learning in Europe.

Her father gladly consented to the change of residence, especially because the interference with the life of his daughter by his ill-tempered wife had now become intolerable. Rather than see Elena Lucrezia suffer a repressive domestic atmosphere, he established her residence in his Paduan palace and provided her with servants, tutors, and female companions.

Among her professors she now enjoyed the lectures of the famous philosopher, Carlo Rinaldini, and those of the celebrated theologians, Fiorelli and Cano.

Elena Lucrezia did not desire academic honors or degrees from the University of Padua. She simply wanted to be away from Venice and continue to learn as much as she could. She was already an oblate of the Benedictine Order. As such she refused three or four advantageous marriages and secretly observed the monastic rule in all its austerity. Under her usual clothes she wore the long scapular of the oblates. To her, her studies were her shield against the outside world; her refuge in her quest for peace and for an inner spiritual life.

Her father, on the contrary, wanted an opportunity for his now famous daughter to give public proof of her extensive and profound learning by defending a theological thesis and by submitting to the rigorous examination at the University of Padua for the Doctor of Theology degree.

His request for this opportunity was most unusual and precedent-breaking. However, Lucrezia, in obedience to his wishes, prepared herself for such a doctorate and in 1667 signed the usual petition for it, addressing it to the rector of the University.

This dignitary enthusiastically approved the request, and all was being made ready for the final formalities and the conferring of the degree. Suddenly the preparation stopped. Serious difficulties had arisen because of the stand taken by the Ecclesiastical Authority. No university had ever conferred the Doctor of Theology on a woman and the Studium of Padua was not going to disregard so venerable a tradition.

The Procurator of San Marco then appealed to Cardinal Gregorio Barbarigo (1625-1697) (now Saint Gregorio Barbarigo), Bishop of Padua and Chancellor of the Theological Faculty of the University. "What? A female doctor and teacher of theology? Never!" replied the cardinal, and he held firmly to that refusal.

Almost a hundred years later, Dr. Samuel Johnson of London, on hearing of a similar curious demand, said: "A woman preaching is like a dog walking on his hind legs; it is not done well, but you are surprised to find it done at all."

In the second half of the twentieth century the Roman Catholic Church abolished its sweeping veto. Today, in Europe, there are many female Doctors of Theology. In Elena Piscopia's day, the Conventual Father Felice Rotondo, a teaching theologian at the University of Padua, remarked: "If the women are permitted to study Theology, why must they be denied the doctorate in that subject?" As his supporters, he cited Duns Scotus (1266-1308), the Jesuit Alfonso Salmeron (1515-1596), and Cornelius a Lapide (1567-1637), Church luminaries.

But Cardinal Barbarigo compromised with Father Rotondo's view, reluctantly. "Woman," he said, "is made for mother-hood, not for learning. However, if the Procurator of San Marco insists, I am willing to modify the point and let his daughter become a Doctor in Philosophy."

Gianbattista Piscopia, accustomed to having his own way, did insist. Realizing that nothing could be done to obtain a doctorate in Theology, he settled for the Doctor of Philosophy degree to be conferred upon his illustrious daughter.

Is it unreasonable at this time to speculate that the final permissiveness of Cardinal Barbarigo, in 1677, might have set a long-range precedent which eventually opened a door to a new era for women of the Roman Catholic world, and in 1970 promoted the doctorate for Saint Theresa of Avila and Saint Catherine of Siena?

The Jesuit Domenico Mondrone in his noted writings re-marked: "The doctorate conferred on these saintly women, though appearing an extraordinary innovation, is not to be contested by any hasty and uninformed journalist. It should rather be considered as a tardy honor bestowed upon two women of genius. May we then be allowed to offer our reader a glamorous and amusing episode apropos of the doctorate of the women of the Church; it is an historic savory curiosity with a significance quite illusive. It is the case of the Venetian Elena Lucrezia Cornaro Piscopia (1646-1684), *the first laureate lady of the world.*" Father Mondrone then succinctly narrates the story of Elena Piscopia.

Conferring of the Doctorate

GIANBATTISTA, having accepted the concession made by Cardinal Barbarigo, urged the University to announce a special convocation for June 5, 1678, to be held in University Hall. At that time pilgrims from all parts of the world were expected in Padua for the approaching (June 13) feast of Saint Anthony, the patron saint of Padua.

Elena Lucrezia, however, did not want the convocation to interfere with the feast of Saint Anthony, nor did she wish to attract too large a concourse for her own academic event. Therefore, she begged her father to delay the ceremony a little. He agreed, and the new date chosen was Saturday morning, June 25, 1678.

Anticipation of the forthcoming convocation filled Elena Lucrezia with dread. She abhorred the whole idea. Her native modesty shrank from so public a display of her amazing learning and cultural understanding. In preparation for the ordeal she prayed incessantly, and received the sacraments as if she were preparing for death.

A half hour before the solemn program began, it was necessary for her confessor to appeal to her humility and urge her to submit. Finally she obeyed, but throughout the whole affair she was so obviously depressed and humiliated that all those who understood and loved her pitied her. And an undercurrent of malicious comment suggested that the father, not the daughter, solicited the degree.

At the last moment, the multitude of guests and spectators was so large that the convocation was transferred from Padua University Hall to the Cathedral of the Blessed Virgin. The most distinguished personalities of Italy together with a great number of scholars from various European universities filled the vast auditorium beyond capacity—all eager to see and hear this first female aspirant to the highest academic honor.

The examiners showed no leniency because of the applicant's age, sex, or family standing. They allowed no superficial inquiry. The powerful prestige of the University was to be augmented here, not diminished. As question after question of the most difficult nature was answered by Elena Lucrezia, with a simple ease and dignity which won all hearts, cheers and applause burst forth repeatedly from the great audience gathered to hear her.

Her brilliant replies, and the profound and varied learning shown in her subsequent scholarly dissertation, compelled the judges to declare that the Philosophy doctorate was hardly an adequate honor for so towering an intellect.

The examination being satisfactorily concluded, Elena Lucrezia Cornaro Piscopia was invested with the *Teacher's Ermine Cape,* received the *Doctor's Ring* on her finger, was crowned with the *Poet's Laurel Crown,* and was elevated to the high dignity of *Magistra et Doctrix Philosphiae—Master and Doctor of Philosophy.* The whole assembly then stood and chanted a glorious *Te Deum.*

Elena Cornaro Piscopia wearing the Ermine Cape, symbol of the *teacher* or *Magistra (Master)* received June 25, 1678.

Antonio Vivani, *Sculptor and Engraver* (1797-1854)
Michele Fanoli, *Designer* (1807-1876)

Museo Civico-Padova, Albano Terme (PD)

Death and Burial

ELENA Lucrezia Cornaro Piscopia did not survive long after her extraordinary achievement. For over thirty years she had secretly served the poor, the sick, the orphans, and all in need, while leading a studious life of penitential austerity. She desired to know and to love more than to live. She died in sanctity on July 25, 1684, at the age of thirty-eight. The entire citizenry of Padua and of Venice gave way to an outburst of sighing and grief. "The saint is dead! The saint is dead!" was the cry throughout both cities.

Her funeral was more like a triumph than a mourning. In accord with her will, she was clothed in the black habit of the Benedictine oblates and laid in a coffin built from the wood of a cypress tree grown in the garden of her Venetian home. She had requested burial in the mortuary of the Benedictine Monks at the Abbey Church of St. Justina, Padua.

But there were those who wanted to ignore her wishes. Her mother, Zanetta, angrily protested what she called an incongruous and inappropriate burial. "My daughter wanted no men in her life. She is not going to be buried with them in death!" she screamed. In spite of Elena's own desire, the parish priest of the parochial Church of Saint Lawrence, Padua, claimed that Elena Lucrezia was a parishioner under his jurisdiction and, therefore, should be buried in her parish church. Her father wanted her buried in the Basilica of Saint Anthony of Padua.

In those days much commotion was often caused by those who strove at all costs to obtain the bones of a saint. Venetians especially distinguished themselves in this business. While they were a great sea power they collected the remains of several saints from various parts of the world. Those they could not get by trade they captured and brought home. Examples are the body of Saint Mark, which they took from Alexandria in Egypt, that of Saint Lucy, which they carried off from Syracuse in Sicily, and the relics of Saint Luke, the Evangelist, which they brought from Constantinople to Padua.

Elena Lucrezia's contemporaries regarded her to be of saintly stature. The contention over her burial was referred to the Bishop of Padua, Cardinal Barbarigo, who had authorized her application for the Doctor of Philosophy. He immediately decided that according to Canon Law the deceased enjoyed the *jus selectionis,* the right to be buried wherever she chose, and, therefore, that her last wish was to be respected and executed.

Thus Zanetta was silenced, and the priest of Saint Lawrence was appeased by being permitted to record her death in his parish register.

The obsequies were held on July 28, 1684, in the Benedictine Abbey Church of Saint Justina, Padua, with an extraordinary gathering of civil and academic dignitaries of Padua, Venice, and other cities. A noble Paduan youth, Campolongo dei Campilongo, representing the University of Padua, delivered the eulogy in Latin.

Two days later the body of Elena Lucrezia Cornaro Piscopia, as she had wished, was laid in the mortuary of Saint Luke's Chapel, adjoining the Abbey Church, the burial place for the abbots and monks of Saint Justina. A zinc tablet was enclosed with the casket, its inscription dealing with the life and work of the first woman in the world to earn a university degree. A marble tablet with further inscription was placed on the tomb. The University of Padua coined a medal commemorating a

woman "not only singular, but unique and without ex-
ample." Shortly after her burial, many universities throughout
Europe held commemorative services in her honor.

Everyone seemed pleased with the tribute paid to Elena
Lucrezia. Her father, however, was not satisfied that all had
been done to honor his famous daughter.

Being an admirer and a benefactor of the Conventual Friars
in charge of the basilica of Saint Anthony in Padua, as Procurator of San Marco he obtained permission from them to erect a
magnificent mausoleum in memory of his daughter in their
basilica. He employed the best sculptor of the time for the
work, and commanded the artist to spare no expense. The
result was a mausoleum extending from a side pilaster almost
to the very middle of the central nave and decorated with
sculptured figures representing Faith, Charity, Purity, and
Death, and the statues of Time, Aristotle, Plato, Democritus,
and Seneca. The mausoleum was topped with a life-sized
statue of Elena Lucrezia, the work of the celebrated sculptor,
Bernardo Tabacco of Bassano, and the insignia *Magistra et
Doctrix.*

The Procurator of San Marco was hopeful, it is said, that the
remains of his daughter might some day be transferred from
Saint Luke's Chapel to the mausoleum in the basilica of
Saint Anthony, but he died without seeing this come to pass.
With his death, it seemed that the memory of Elena Lucrezia
Cornaro Piscopia disappeared, for a time, into oblivion.

In 1727, forty-three years after her death, with the consent of
the Cornaro family, the empty mausoleum was dismantled
and removed from the basilica of Saint Anthony. It had
occupied too much space in the central nave, where it ob-
structed the view of the main altar. That year, the bust of
Elena Piscopia, with a laudatory inscription, was placed, in
lieu of the dismantled mausoleum, in the center of the
basilica of Saint Anthony—where it may still be seen. Tabacco's

End Wall decorated for ceremonies to honor
Elena Cornaro Piscopia after her death

baroque statue was, in 1772, given to the University, at the expense and through the good offices of the noble Lady Caterina Dolfin, herself a Benedictine oblate. This is the statue I admired in 1936. No one knows what happened to the dismantled mausoleum, built at a cost of more than a million ducats.

Although some of the literary works of the learned Doctor of Philosophy have come down to us, the vast mass of her manuscripts was dispersed. Since, at the time of her death, she was considered more a saint than just a person of great learning, all her belongings were sought out and divided by pious relatives and friends who considered them precious relics. What remains of her voluminous literary papers are translations from the Spanish, Latin, and Greek. We have a few of her poems in Italian, Greek, and Latin, all harmonious and original. Her surviving letters, written in several languages, are interesting and informative. They reveal her noble character and highlight her charm, simplicity, sincerity, and determination. Her Latin letters have often been published to prove that their author is rightfully numbered among the best Latinists of her time.

Present Day Revival and Recognition

For nearly two hundred years the phenomenal Elena Piscopia was lost in silence. But in 1895, the Abbess of the English Benedictine Nuns stationed in Rome, Lady Mathilde Pynsent, rescued her memory. She went to Padua, identified the grave on the Epistle side of the altar in the monk's mortuary at Saint Justina, and had it opened. The remains of her illustrious sister were officially recognized by both civil and ecclesiastical authorities. Then the English Abbess had the remains enclosed in a new lead casket and replaced in the same grave.

All those present at this ceremony wrote their names on the lid of the new coffin. They are Mechtildis Pynsent, Abbess, O.S.B.; Dom Maurus Watson, Postulator, O.S.B.; Jacobus A. Campbell, Rector of the Scottish College in Rome; Carlo Ferraris, Rector of the University of Padua; Don Marino Frattin, O.S.B., Superior of Saint George Major in Venice; Don Domenico Puller, Parish Priest; Gaetano D. Varda for the Municipality of Padua; and Don Giovanni Campius, Delegate of the Bishop of Padua. The date is added: Wednesday, September 11, 1895, 12 o'clock noon. They placed a new slab of marble on the grave, bearing a long biographical inscription.

On her return to Rome, the Abbess Pynsent published, in 1896, an interesting book, *The Life of Helen Lucretia Cornaro Piscopia*. The book, in English and very readable, has long been out of print.

Perhaps this book furnished the inspiration for the theme of the great stained glass window in the Gothic Library at Vassar College, Poughkeepsie, New York, a library donated in 1896 by Mrs. Frederick F. Thompson in memory of her husband, who had been a trustee of Vassar. This magnificent stained glass window shows the Cornaro, thesis in hand, before her examiners, who are about to invest her with the ermine lined scholar's cape and the laurel wreath, symbols of the doctorate.

The impression made by that artistic window brought knowledge of Elena Lucrezia to the University of Pittsburgh. While a student at Vassar, Ruth Crawford (Mitchell), class of 1912, spent many hours studying beneath the great window in the Vassar library. Some years after graduation, when she became a lecturer in sociology at the University of Pittsburgh, she still remembered and wished to share with her associates her admiration for the Cornaro story and its significance in the academic world.

About the year 1930 Mrs. Mitchell realized her wish. The University of Pittsburgh was building the Cathedral of Learning, the famous Gothic tower, a classroom and office building. On the first floor of this unique structure large classrooms were placed at the disposal of the nationalities represented in the citizenry of Pittsburgh and in the student body. Mrs. Mitchell was entrusted to direct the work, in which each group would assume responsibility for the furnishing and decoration of a classroom, in authentic national style.

Mrs. Mitchell organized a committee of prominent Italo-Americans with a special Italian Women's Committee headed by Mrs. Samuel Molinari. The Italian Classroom was furnished according to the monastic design of Mrs. Margherita Chiari Langer of Florence and dedicated to the Italian scholar Elena Lucrezia Cornaro Piscopia. The celebrated portrait painter Giovanni Romagnoli of Bologna was invited to come to Pittsburgh to decorate the rear wall of the classroom with a mural depicting Elena Lucrezia Cornaro Piscopia, the first woman in the world to receive the degree, Doctor of Philosophy.

This graceful and charming mural was unveiled in 1949. Today, the Italian Classroom is an oasis of beauty and peacefulness, and a very useful university classroom. At its dedication an orator remarked: "History records many famous intellectual women. We can boast of a Manto, celebrated in astronomy; an Erinna and Saffo in poetry; a Diotime in philosophy; a Hildegarde in theology; a Zenobia and an Amalasunta in the Latin, Greek, Hebrew, and Egyptian tongues; Saint Theresa of Avila; Saint Catherine of Siena; and a hundred more celebrated women; but there is only one woman who accumulated in herself all that we admire individually among these, and she is Elena Lucrezia Cornaro Piscopia. One of her contemporaries, Doctor Francesco Gabiati, said, 'She was, as it were, a Hydra of Learning and Virtue, for she professed seven sciences, and had a perfect knowledge of seven of the most notable languages.'"

Since then, the memory of Elena Piscopia has not only been kept alive, it has continued to grow. Through the most benevolent effort of the Abbot Don Innocenzo DeAngelis and the oblates of Saint Justina in Padua, with Mrs. Ruth Crawford Mitchell of Pittsburgh, a movement is now under way to restore the crypt in the monks' mortuary at Saint Justina, where Elena Lucrezia is buried, and to restore the tomb for her coffin. A world-wide investigation on behalf of the Institute of History, University of Padua, has established the primacy of Elena Lucrezia as the first woman Doctor of Philosophy.

A cooperative effort, with activity in Italy and in the United States, is under way to enlist women graduates of universities to help prepare for the Tercentenary of the first granting of the Doctor of Philosophy degree to a woman. This will be solemnized in 1978 in Padua and throughout the world.

NICOLA FUSCO 1971

[47]

Bibliography

This bibliography was compiled by Dr. Maria Tonzig, a graduate of the University of Padua and author of *The Romanesque Gothic Basilica in Padua,* articles in the Bulletin of the Civic Museum of Padua, 1929-1932. It was prepared in 1972 for Professor Paolo Sambin, director of the Institute for the History of the University of Padua, whose three-year period of research has documented the Cornaro Primacy announced on October 14, 1972, at the 750th anniversary of the University of Padua.

The editing of Dr. Tonzig's Italian Bibliography and the listing of several additional items in all categories of manuscript and printed material have been compiled by John Halmaghi, Hillman Library Bibliographer, University of Pittsburgh.

List of Abbreviations

Card.—Cardinal   lat.—Latin   s.d.—No date
Cod.—Codex   n.d.—No Date   s.n.t.—No Publisher
fasc. Fascicule   n. num.—Not Numbered

Symbols Used in This Bibliography

BM   British Museum—London.
BN   Bibliothèque Nationale—Paris.
CBPac   Pacific School of Religion, Berkeley, California.
CLU   University of California at Los Angeles, Los Angeles, California.
CLgA   Alma College, Los Gatos, California.
CSt   Stanford University Libraries, Stanford, California.
CU   University of California, Berkeley, California.
CtW   Wesleyan University, Middletown, Connecticut.
CtY   Yale University, New Haven, Connecticut.

CtY-D	Yale University, Divinity School Library, New Haven, Conn.
CtY-M	Yale University, Medical School Library, New Haven, Conn.
DCU	Catholic University of America Library, District of Columbia.
DFo	Folger Shakespeare Library, District of Columbia.
DHN	Holy Name College Library, District of Columbia.
DLC	U.S. Library of Congress, District of Columbia.
DLC-P4	U.S. Library of Congress, Priority 4 Collection, D.C.
DM	U.S. Library of Congress, U.S. Bureau of Mines Library. (Library integrated with DI), District of Columbia.
DNLM	U.S. National Library of Medicine, District of Columbia.
FU	University of Florida, Gainesville, Florida.
ICJ	John Crerar Library, Chicago, Illinois.
ICN	Newberry Library, Chicago, Illinois.
ICU	University of Chicago, Chicago, Illinois.
IU	University of Illinois, Urbana, Illinois.
KU	University of Kansas, Lawrence, Kansas.
LNHT	Tulane University Library, New Orleans, Louisiana.
LU	Louisiana State University, Baton Rouge, Louisiana.
MB	Boston Public Library, Boston, Massachusetts.
MH	Harvard University, Cambridge, Massachusetts.
MH-AH	Andover-Harvard Theological Library, Harvard University, Cambridge, Massachusetts.
MWelC	Wellesley College, Wellesley, Massachusetts.
MdBJ	Johns Hopkins University, Baltimore, Maryland.
MdU	University of Maryland, College Park, Maryland.
MiEM	Michigan State University, East Lansing, Michigan.
MiU	University of Michigan, Ann Arbor, Michigan.
MnCS	St. John's University, Collegeville, Minnesota.
MnU	University of Minnesota, Minneapolis, Minnesota.
MoSW	Washington University, St. Louis, Missouri.
NIC	Cornell University, Ithaca, New York.
NN	New York Public Library, New York, New York
NNC	Columbia University, New York, New York.
NNGr	Grolier Club Library, New York, New York.
NNH	Hispanic Society of America, New York, New York.
NRU	University of Rochester, Rochester, New York.
NcD	Duke University, Durham, North Carolina.
NcU	University of North Carolina, Chapel Hill, North Carolina.
NjP	Princeton University, Princeton, New Jersey.
NjPT	Princeton Theological Seminary, Princeton, New Jersey.

NjR	Rutgers—The State University, New Brunswick, New Jersey.
OCU	University of Cincinnati, Cincinnati, Ohio.
ODW	Ohio Wesleyan University, Delaware, Ohio.
OrCS	Oregon State University Library, Corvallis, Oregon.
OrU	University of Oregon, Eugene, Oregon.
PBm	Bryn Mawr College, Bryn Mawr, Pennsylvania.
PLatS	Saint Vincent College and Archabbey, Latrobe, Pennsylvania.
PP	Free College of Philadelphia, Philadelphia, Pennsylvania.
PPC	College of Physicians of Philadelphia, Philadelphia, Pa.
PPL	Library Company of Philadelphia, Pennsylvania.
PPLT	Lutheran Theological Seminary, Krauth Memorial Library, Philadelphia, Pennsylvania.
PPLas	La Salle College, Philadelphia, Pennsylvania.
PPULC	Union Library Catalogue of Pennsylvania, Philadelphia, Pa.
PU	University of Pennsylvania, Philadelphia, Pennsylvania.
RPB	Brown University, Providence, Rhode Island.

Works by Elena Lucrezia Cornaro Piscopia

A. *Manuscripts*

1. Discorso accademico sopra la Madonna della Neve recitato nell'Accademia degli Infecondi in S. Carlo de'Catinari a die 4 agosto 1967 dall'illustrissima signora Elena Lucrezia Cornara Piscopia nobile dama veneziana. Città del Vaticano, Biblioteca Apostolica Vaticana, Cod. Barberiniano, latino 4502, ff. 98-103.

2. Lettera della nobile donna Elena Cornara al nobile uomo cavaliere procuratore Antonio Grimani. Venezia, s.d. in indirizzo esterno, Biblioteca del Civico Museo Correr, Ms. Morosini-Grimani, b. 442, XVII.

3. Lettere della Cornaro scritte al Card. Barberini dal 18 Aprile 1671 al 18 dicembre 1677. Città del Vaticano, Bibl. Apostolica Vaticana, Cod. Barberiniano, lat. 6562, ff. 1692-1694 v.

B. *Edited or Printed Works*

1. Dedica alla veneta nobilità, Poesie greche e latine, Elogi ("Septilingui laudatione commendat") al P. Luprani. *Seconda corona intrecciata da vari letterati* . . . Venezia, Bosio, 1675. Dedica di 4 p.n. num. ep. 45-64.

2. Elogia, Epistolae. Accademia degli Infecondi. Roma. *Poesie de' signori Accademici Infecondi di Roma.* Venezia, Hertz, 1684. Appendice p. 31-47, 49-53.

3. Epigramma Greco-Latino. *Apantismatologia ovvero Raccoglimento poetico dei più fioriti ingegni* . . . Padova, Cadorino, 1668. p. 7-10.

4. Epigramma Greco-Latino. *Antonio Dragoni. Orazione.* Udine, Schiratti, 1683, p. 138-139.

5. Epigrammi Latini. Accademia degli Infecondi. Roma. *Poesie de' signori Accademici Infecondi di Roma.* Venezia, Pezzana, 1678. p. 341.

6. *Helenae Lucretiae* . . . *Corneliae Piscopiae* . . . *opera quae quidem haberi potuerunt,* etc. Edited by B. Bacchini, with a life of the author. Parma, Rosati, 1688. Stampa ritratto a 22 anni del Langlois. p. 51-136, 143-145, 151-158, 175-310. BM BN

7. Lettera. *Caroli Renaldini. Commercium epistolicum.* Patavii, Frambotti, 1682, part 3, p. 65.

8. *Lettera, ovvero Colloquio di Cristo Nostro Redentore all'anima devota,* composta da Giovanni Laspergio cartusiano . . . Tradotta dallo spagnolo in italiano da Elena Cornaro. La Cornaro dedica la traduzione al Padre Oliva e presenta il libro al lettore. Segue un epigramma latino-spagnolo scritto dal Macedo in onore della stessa Cornaro e la traduzione del testo. Venetia, Giuliani, 1669. Dedica p. 7-10, prefazione 9 p.n. num., epigramma 2 p.n. num., traduzione p. 11-162.

9. *Lettera, ovvero Colloquio di Cristo* . . . Venetia, Giuliani, 1673. Dedica p. 5-8, prefazione p. 9-12, epigramma p. 13-14, traduzione p. 15-162.

10. *Lettera, ovvero Colloquio di Cristo* . . . Venetia, Hertz, 1681. Dedica p. 3-6, presentazione p. 7-11, traduzione p. 14-204.

11. *Lettera, ovvero Colloquio di Cristo* . . . Venetia, Hertz, 1706. Prefazione p. 3-6, epigramma p. 7-8, traduzione p. 9-192.

12. Lettere. *Cristoforo Ivanovich, Minerva al tavolino.* Venezia, Pezzana, 1688. Parte I, p. 84-90, 94-96, 99; parte II, p. 195-210.

13. Ostastichon. *Accademia patavina di scienze, lettere ed arti. Composizioni delli signori Accademici Ricovrati.* Padova, Frambotti, 1678. p. 57.

14. Poesie. *Gozzi, Luisa (Bergalli) Gozzi, Contessa. Componimenti Poetici delle più illustri rimatrici* . . ., Venezia, Mora, 1726 v.2, p. 17-26, 169. DFo PU ICN CtY BM BN

Works about Elena Lucrezia Cornaro Piscopia

A. *Manuscripts*

1. Annuncio della morte di Elena Lucrezia Cornaro Piscopia. Lettera di Giacobelli a Borghi, 5 agosto 1684. Città del Vaticano, Archivio Segreto, S.S., Venezia 127, ff. 532 r—533 v, 540 r.

2. Atti e parti. Rimozione deposito di Elena Cornaro Piscopia nella chiesa del Santo, 1727, 14 luglio. Padova, Archivio antico della Ven. Arca del Santo, Ms. vol. 28 (XXVII n. vecchia) ff. 129 r, 131 v.

3. Atto di nascita di Corner Gio. Battista Guglielmo di Girolamo q. Giacomo Alvise e di Catterina Tileno di

Guglielmo, n. 1 aprile 1613. Venezia, Arch. di Stato di Venezia, Ms. Cassetta Nascite 168, fasc. VII, 185.

4. Bartolomeo Dotti. Sonetti. In morte della nobil donna signora Elena Cornara Piscopia posseditrice di varie lingue. Venezia, Biblioteca del Civico Museo Correr, Ms. Correr, 872, f. 45.

5. Copie delle fedi di battesimo di Elena Cornaro e del fratello Girolamo:
—1825, 12 aprile: della chiesa parrocchiale di S. Luca di Venezia. Venezia, Biblioteca del Civico Museo Correr, Ms. Correr 2039, f. 1577.

6. Cornaro (famiglia). Raccolta di scritture e suppliche di Gio. Battista Cornaro di S. Luca Procuratore di S. Marco per poter usare il titolo di cavaliere del Regno di Cipro concesso in perpetuo alla sua famiglia da Pietro Lusignano Re di Cipro e alloggiato nel palazzo di S. Luca nel 1363. Venezia, Archivio di Stato di Venezia Ms. Misc. Codici I—Storia Veneta, B. 149 (già codici Brera 58), Dal 1377 al 1691, ff. 55 n. num. e 4 ff. a stampa.

7. Cornaro (famiglia). Stemma nel Palazzo d'Asolo del 1489. Venezia. Biblioteca del Civico Museo Correr. Ms. cod. Gradenigo. Acquarello di Grevembroch, n. 65, vol. 1, c. LXXXI, n. 243.

8. Corner.—Palazzo a San Luca. Venezia. Bibl. del Civico Museo Correr. Ms. P.D., c. 7-55/51.

9. Corner Piscopia famiglia. Informazioni sopra il titolo del cavalierato. Venezia. Bibl. del Civico Museo Correr. Ms. Cicogna 3417. fascicolo Corner-Piscopia, 16 ff. non num.

10. Corner Piscopia famiglia. Sec. XVIII. Arma Cornaro dalla Piscopia. (Descrizione dello stemma). Venezia, Biblioteca del Civico Museo Correr, Ms. P.D. c. 816/10, 6 ff. n. num.

11. Corner Piscopia—Palazzo. Appunti del prof. Lorenzetti per la storia del palazzo Corner-Piscopia. Venezia, Bibl. del Civico Museo Correr, Ms. P.D., c. 2759, XVII.

12. Cronaca Savina. Visite dell'Imperatore . . . dal 1356 as 1401. Venezia, Bibl. Museo civico Correr, Ms. Cicogna 3751, ff. 240, 247, 355.

13. Descrizione delle armi e delle insegne della facciata del palazzo del N.H. Giovanni Battista Corner Piscopia. Venezia, Archivio di Stato di Venezia, Avogaria, Ms. B. 3820, misc. +4 p. a stampa n. num.

14. Diversorum II, ab anno 1675 usque 1686.
—1678, 22 iunii: Presentatio in philosophia nobilis virginis venetae dominae Helenae Lucretiae Corneliae.
—die 25 dicti de mane: examen et approbatio. Padova, Archivio Curia Vescovile di Padova, Diversorum II, vol. 81, f. 103.

15. Emmanuele Antonio Cicogna. Copia del manoscritto di Giovanni Scardova: Storia compendiosa della vita di Elena Lucrezia Cornara Piscopia . . . fatta nel 1818 con l'aggiunta del documento per la benedizione del mausoleo nella Basilica del Santo. Venezia, Biblioteca del Civico Museo Correr. Monoscritto Cicogna 2134, ff. 147 n. num.

16. Ephemeridi Cartharie; anno 1685, Academia Infecundorum solemnis, Domenica 15 luglio: F(unzione) in lode della signora Elena Cornara Piscopia. Roma, Archivio di Stato di Roma, Fondo Carthari Febei, Ms. 92, ff. 184 v, 185, 186 r.

17. Gaspare Cantu' Ottaviani. Descrizione della funzione in cui venne conferita la laurea alla nobil donna Elena Cornaro Piscopia il 25 giugno 1678. Padova, Biblioteca del Civico Museo, Ms. B.P. 126, XIV.

18. Ghero. Stampe:
    N. 1738: Stemma con didascalia;
    N. 1744: Albero genealogico per il Doge Marco Corner
    con stemma del 1673 (non risulta la famiglia
    Corner Piscopia).
    Venezia, Bibl. del civico Museo Correr, Ghero-Stampe,
    4 parte I.

19. Giambattista Cornaro Piscopia. Sue suppliche per diventar
    procuratore di S. Marco nel 1649. Venezia, Bibl. del Civico
    Museo Correr, Ms. misc. Cicogna 1108, ff. 69, 111, 403-409.

20. Giambattista Cornaro Piscopia. Suppliche per l'ammissione
    dei figli al libro d'oro:
    1659, 4 agosto = negative
    1659,   settembre = negative
    1664   ”
    1664,   marzo = positive.
    Venezia, Bibl. del Civico Museo Correr, Misc., Ms. Correr
    1110, ff. 1-4.

21. Giornale "A" Delle Nobilissime Accademie Dei Ricovrati,
    dal 1599 al 1694:
    —1669, 11 febbraio: aggregazione senza supplica quale
    membro dell'accademia, f. 209.
    —L'accademia invia alla Cornaro il decreto di nomina, f.
    211
    —1669, 29 marzo: La Cornaro ringrazia il Principe e gli
    accademici, f. 211
    —1678, 15 luglio: Accademia pubblica in lode della illustris-
    sima Elena Cornara dottorata in filosofia, f. 290
    —1684, 1 settembre: Accademia pubblica in funere della
    signora Elena Lucretia Cornaro Piscopia, f. 341
    —1684, 14 settembre: nell'accademia di detto giorno ven-
    gono lette le lettere, riportate in copia, scritte il 5 settembre
    da Gio. Battista Cornaro al Principe; il 6 settembre dal

Principe a Gio. Battista Cornaro. Nella stessa tornata il Principe comunica le decisione di far stampare, a sue spese, tutte le composizioni recitate in funere di Elena Cornaro, ff. 342-343r. Padova, Archivio dell'Accademia Patavina, Giornale "A" Delle Nobilissime Accademie Dei Ricovrati, Ms. senza segnatura, ff. 209, 211, 290, 341, 342, 343 r.

22. Giovanni Scardova. Storia compendiosa della vita di Elena Lucrezia Cornaro Piscopia dama veneta addottorata in filosofia ed aggregata al Sacro Collegio de' Filosofi e Medici. Padova, Biblioteca del Civico Museo, Ms. B.P. 125, I, cartaceo di ff. 65.

23. Girolamo Alessandro Capellari. Il Campidoglio Veneto. Venezia, Biblioteca Marciana, I Ms. It. Cl. VII, n. 15, 8304, ff. 326 v, 327, 328, 332 v.

24. Giuseppe Gennari. Saggio storico sopra le Accademie di Padova. Cap. VI, nota n. 15. Padova. Biblioteca del Civico Museo. B.P. 6117 I. Ms. ff. n. num.

25. Gregorio Barbarigo, Card. Lettere degli anni 1677-1680. Venezia, Biblioteca Seminario Patriarcale, Ms. Fondo Barbarigo, pv. Donà delle Rose, VII-9, ff. 303-304, 309, 319-320, 324, 336, 344-345, 353, 357, 368-369, 387-388.

26. Grossi, Carlo. Sacre ariose cantate, Bologna, Magni detto Gardano, 1663. vol. 4.

27. Index quartus actorum sacri collegi . . . Paduae, 1678 ianuari, 1681, augusti:
—1678, 22 iunii, presentatio in philosophia illustrissimae dominae Elenae Lucretiae Corneliae Piscopiae, f. 24 v.
—1678, 24 iunii, puncta pro examine in philosophia, f. 25r.
—1678, 25 iunii, examen et approbatio in philosophia more nobilium illustrissimae et excellentissimae Elena Lucretiae Corneliae Piscopiae, ff. 25 rv, 26 rv. Padova, Archivio Antico dell'Università di Padova, Ms. 365, ff. 24v, 25, 26 rv.

28. Informazione del titolo del cavalierato di Cipro. Venezia, Bibl. Marciana, Ms. It. Cl. XI, Cod. CLXXXIII = 7362, fasc. II, ff. 7 n. num.

29. Iscrizioni sparse per la città (di Venezia), parte I, n. 414—parte II, f. 5 r. Venezia, Bibl. del Civico Museo Correr, Ms. cod. Cicogna 2017.

30. Joanni Grevembroch. Gli abiti de' Veneziani di qualsiasi età con diligenza raccolti e dipinti nel sec. XVIII, p. 49, 156. Venezia, Bibl. del Civico Museo Correr, Ms. Cod. Gradenigo 49.

31. Joanni Grevembroch. Varie venete curiosità sacre e profane, 1755, tav. XXXIII, n. 103: lo stemma di Federico Cornaro sopra il di lui palagio di S. Luca, fregiato dell'insegna di Pietro Lusignano Re di Cipro allorquando ivi alloggiò in Venezia, l'anno 1363. Venezia, Bibl. del Civico Museo Correr, Ms. Cod. Gradenigo-Dolfin, I, 65.

32. Lettera di Giambattista Cornaro, Venezia, li 27 febbraio 1679. Venezia, Archivio di Stato di Venezia, Misc. Ms. Busta 490, ff. 4 n. num.

33. Lettere de' riformatori dello studio di Padova scritte ai rettori et altri de 11 giugno 1677 fin 23 febraio 1679.
—1677, 18 ottobre: Alli rettori di Padova, disposizioni per rendere più solenne possibile la funzione della laurea in teologia, f. n. num.
—1678, 16 giugno: idem per la laurea in filosofia, f. n. num.
—1679, 7 febraio: idem per proibire il laurearsi ad altre donne, n. num.
Venezia, Archivio di Stato di Venezia, Riformatori dello studio di Padova, b. 75 sub anno.

34. Lettere di abilitazione o miscellanea, copia della lettera del 16 giugno 1678. Padova, Archivio Antico dell'Università di Padova, Ms. 716. f. 121 v.

35. Lettere di abilitazione per dottorati more nobilium e in Collegio Veneto. Dottorato di Lucrezia Cornaro Piscopia.
—1678, 16 giugno: copia della lettera originale segnata al No. 9.
—1679, 7 febbraio: copia della lettera originale segnata al No. 10.
Padova, Archivio Antico dell'Università di Padova, Ms. 707 O 57, f. 101.

36. Liber Defunctorum, ad usum ecclesiae parochialis S. Laurentii de Padua 1670-1693:
—1684, 25 luglio: Atto di morte di Elena Cornaro Piscopia.
Padova, Archivio Curia Vescovile di Padova, Ms. 31, ff. 114v, 115, 116 r.

37. Libro dei morti dal 1680 al 1685:
—1684, 26 luglio: Illustrissima et eccellentissima signora Elena Lucrezia Cornaro Piscopia.
Padova, Archivio di Stato di Padova, Ufficio Sanità di Padova, Ms. 483, sub voce E.

38. Marco Barbaro. Arbori de' Patrizii Veneti. Venezia, Archivio di Stato di Venezia, III, Ms. 29 aprile—6 luglio 1743, ff. 17-27, Misc. Codd. 896.

39. Marco Barbaro. Discendenze Patrizie. Venezia, Biblioteca del Civico Museo Correr, Ms. Cicogna XI—E 2/2, III, ff. 11 v, 12, 13 14 r. E' in parte diverso dal Ms. s.c. al N. 38.

40. Notizie su Elena Lucrezia Cornaro Piscopia. Venezia, Biblioteca del Civico Museo, Ms. Cicogna 3417, V. fasc. Corner Piscopia Elena Lucrezia, 2 ff. n. num.

41. Opuscula varia latina et italica. Pro doctoratu in sacra theologia nobilis et doctissimae virginis Elenae Corneliae Piscopiae Venetae. Padova, Biblioteca Antoniana, Ms. XXII, 588, fasc. 8, 72 ff. n. num.

42. Origine Dei Cornari. (poche righe). Venezia, Bibl. del Civico Museo Correr, Ms. Gradenigo-Dolfin 130, f. 24 v.

43. Origine Dei Cornari. (poche righe e 5 stemmi). Venezia, Bibl. del Civico Museo Correr, Ms. Gradenigo-Dolfin 131, ff. 61-r, 62 v.

44. Origine delle famiglie aggregate alla nobiltà veneta per via di offerto assieme alle suppliche. Venezia, Bibl. del Civico Museo Correr, I, Ms. Cicogna 1213, ff. 23 v.—24, 197 v.—200 r, 200 r-202 r., 203v-205v., 206 r.-207 v.

45. Pasquale Pucciani. Araldo veneziano nel quale sono esposte . . . Stemmi Corner: n. 40, 41, 62, 63, 64, 65, 68, 71, 72, 73, 74, 78, 101, 102, 103, 105, 106, 107, 108, 109, 173. Venezia, Bibl. del Civico Museo Correr, Ms. Gradenigo-Dolfin 150.

46. Piero Foscarini, iun. Notizie di famiglie patrizie. Venezia Biblioteca Marciana, Ms. It. VII, 183 (8161), ff. 108-189.

47. Pietro Paolo Ormanico. Cenni sulla famiglia Cornaro. Brescia, Bibl, Civica Queriniana, F. VI. 5. ma 26a.

48. Poesie eroiche di diversi autori. Il sole coronato dal sole nel mirable dottorato dell'illustrissima signora Cornaro Piscopia figliuola di S.E. illustrissima Gio. Battista procuratore di S. Marco. Venezia. Biblioteca del Civico Museo Correr, Ms. Cicogna 1216, ff. 104-107, strofe 14.

49. Privilegi, titoli, concessioni, feudi goduti dalla famiglia Corner Piscopia specialmente nel Regno di Cipro. (rifà la storia riportando alcuni documenti). Venezia, Bibl. del Civico Museo Correr, Ms. P.D. 83. c., Cartaceo sec. XVIII, ff. n. num.

50. Registro battesimi dal 1633 al 1647. 1647 adi 6 Zugno 7/, Elena Lucretia fia dell'illustrissimo . . . Venezia, Archivio della parrocchia di S. Luca, Ms. 2 sub voce E.

51. Relazione delle famiglie nobili di Venezia, parte II, sec. XVIII. (Poche righe sulla famiglia Cornaro Piscopia). Venezia, Bibl. del Civico Museo Correr, Ms. Cicogna 2166, ff. n. num.

52. Relazione di una tornata accademica sostenuta da Elena Cornaro Piscopia a Venezia nel suo palazzo il 30 maggio 1677 Città Vaticano' Bibl. Apostolica Vaticana, Ms. Ottob. lat. 2479 (I), ff. 55, 1677, Venezia, 5 giugno.

53. Rezzonico, Traduzione della Medea edea dedicata all'Ill ... mo Signor Giambatista Cornaro Piscopia. Venezia, Bibl. del Civico Museo Correr, Ms. Cicogna 618, f. 7.

54. Ricognizione della salma e inizio processo di beatificazione:
—1895, 8 settembre; richiesta del permesso per la ricognizione della salma della Cornaro.
—1895, 9 settembre: il municipio concede il permesso.

—1895, 11 settembre, ore 12: esumazione e ricognizione della salma.
—Si notifica che subito dopo la morte il Vescovo ha dato inizio al processo per la beatificazione della Cornaro.
Padova, Archivio della Curia Vescovile di Padova, Ms. Fondo Processi per Beatificazioni e Canonizzazioni, b. II, 7 ff. n. num.

55. S. Antonio Confessore, 1684, adì 12 agosto:
—Supplica presentata dal dottor Calafatti a nome dell'ecc. mo proc. Cornaro Piscopia per edificare il deposito dedicato alla figlia nella basilica del Santo. Padova, Archivio di Stato di Padova, Ms. 200, ff. 160, 161.

56. Storia ed alberi della famiglia Corner. Indice XVIII. Venezia Bibl. del Civico Museo Correr, Ms. Correr 1465, f. 404 n. 241; f. 405 n. 263; f. 410 n. 349.

[61]

B. *Printed Works—17th Century*

1. Accademia degli Infecondi. Roma. *Applausi accademici alla laurea filosofica dell'illustrissima* signora Elena Lucrezia Cornara Piscopia, accademica Infeconda. Composti e raccolti dall' Accademia stessa. Roma, Giacomo Dragondelli, 1679. 112 p. BM

2. Accademia degli Infeconda. Roma. *Poesie de' signoria accademici infecondi di Roma.* Venezia, Hertz, 1684. Appendix p. 36, 48.

3. Accademia degli Infecondi, Roma. *Le pompe funebri celebrate da' signori accademici infecondi di Roma per la morte dell'illustrissima Signora Elena Lucrezia Cornara Piscopia, accademica detta l'inalterabile.* Dedicate alla sereniss. Republica di Venezia. Padova, Per il Cadorino, 1686. 188 p. 6 Stampe di Thomas Cardanus. IU NN CtY BM

4. Accademia Patavina di scienze, lettere ed arti. *Compositioni degli accademici ricovrati per la morte della nobile donna, signora Elena Lucrezia Cornaro Piscopia* dedicata all'Eccellenza del signor Gianbattista suo padre Procuratore di S. Marco dal conte Alessandro Abb. De Lazzara Principe dell'Accademia. Padova, Frambotti, 1684. p. 1-100.

5. Accademia Patavina di scienze, lettere ed arti. *Epigramma in lode di Elena Cornaro* publicato col ritratio allorchè per acclamazione fu aggregata all'Accademia dei Ricoverati in Padova. s.n.t., 1669.

6. *Acta eruditorum* anno 1682-1731. Lipsiae, Grossium & Gledit-schium, 1682-1731. v. 1-50, v. 8, p. 1-5. DLC PPC PPL CtY NNH NNC KU

7. Bacchini, Benedetto. *Helenae Lucretiae . . . Corneliae Piscopiae . . . opera quae quidem haberi potuetunt,* etc. Edited by B. Bacchini, with a life of the author. Parma, Rosati, 1688. 310 p. Stampa ritratto a 22 anni del Langlois. p. 1-48, 139-142, 146-150, 159-174. BM BN

8. Bonini, Filippo Maria. *Il Ciro politico*. Venezia, N. Pezzana, 1668. 2 v. in 1. v. 2 249. BM

9. Bottalino, Giambattista. *Ode per la morte di Elena Lucrezia Cornaro Piscopia deplorata dall'Accademia degli Erranti di Brescia*. Brescia, Turlino, 1685. p. 16-20.

10. Bronckhorst, Otto. *La dama di lettere:* applausi ad Elena Cornaro Piscopia accademica Ricovrata, dedicata alle dame di Padova. Padova, Stamperia dell'Università dei Legisti, 15 Luglio 1678. 9 p. n. num.

11. Busino, Pietro. *Elogio in lingua greca e latina*. Venezia, Mottali, 1669.

12. Calafatti, Giorgio. *Trattato sopra la peste*. Venezia, Hertz, 1682. 259 p. p. 152. DLC

13. Caro, Francesco. *Orazione funebre al catafalco di Elena Lucrezia Cornaro Piscopia, filosofa laureata*. Padova, Frambotti, 1684. 13 p. n. num.

14. Caro, Francesco. *Oratio parentalis Helenae Lucretiae Corneliae Piscopiae habita in templo S. Justinae*. Anno 1684, die 26 Iuli. Patavii, Frambotti, 1684. 11 p. n. num.

15. *Descrizione delle figure contenute nel deposito fatto erigere nella chiesa di S. Antonio in memoria di Elena Lucrezia Cornaro Piscopia*. s.n.t., 169. v.4, fasc. VI, 4 p. n. num.

16. Deza, Massimiliano. *Vita di Helena Lucretia Cornara Piscopia*. Venezia, Bosio, 1686. 131 p. e Ritratto. BM BN

17. Deza, Massimiliano. *Vita di Elena Lucrezia Cornaro*. Venezia, Casamara, 1687. 112 p. e Ritratto Diverso; sembra della Piccini Ma è un pò diverso e non è firmato.

18. Deza, Massimiliano. *Vita di Elena Lucrezia Cornaro*. Venezia, Bosio, 1692. p. 1-131, 4 p. n. num. e un altro ritratto di suor Isabella Piccini.

19. Eliseo da Gesu' e Maria. *Effectus divinae Gratiae,* Venezia, 1677.

20. Fabri, Giovanni Battista. *La conchiglia celeste ;* elogii di principi ed uomini illustri d'Italia. Venezia, 1690. 7 pts. p. 33-38. BM BN

21. Fiorelli, Giacomo. *Detti e fatti memorabili del senato e patrizii veneti.* Venezia, Combi, 1672. p. 282-283. IU BM BN

22. Fontana, Carlo. *La fatalità del Savio,* per la morte di Elena Lucrezia Cornaro Piscopia. Brescia, Rizzardi, 1685. p. 1-84.

23. Franchini, Giovanni. *Bibliosofie e memorie letterarie.* Modena, Soliani, 1693. p. 606-607. BM BN

24. Frugoni, Francesco Fulvio. *L'Eroina intrepida.* Venezia, 1673. 4 vol. v. 4, p. 299-300.

25. Frugoni, Francesco Fulvio. *De'ritratti critici abbozzati e contornati da Francesco Fulvio Frugoni.* Venetia, Combi et La Nou, 1669. 3 vol. v. III, p. 262-277. CtY CU BM BN

26. *Giornale de'letterati per tutto l'anno 1688.* Parma, Rosati, 1688. p. 34-36.

27. *Giornale Veneto XVIII de'Litterati.* I Dicembre 1675. Venezia, Valvasense, 1676. p. 137-138.

28. Giudice, Giovanni Battista del. *Poesie sacre e morali.* Palermo, 1673. p. 321.

29. Hottinger, Johann Heinrich. *Historiae Ecclesiasticae Novi Testamenti* . . . Tomus VI: Saeculi XVI, pars II. Tiguri, J.H. Hambergeri, impensis M. Schufelbergeri, 1664. BN

30. Ivanovich, Cristoforo. *Minerva al tavolino.* Venezia, Pezzana 1688. 2 vol. Vol. I, pp. 90-93, 97-98, 100-101, 264, Vol. II, p. 211-212, 261, 375-382, 384-386, 410-411, 426-427, 429.

31. Leti, Gregorio. *L'Italia regnante.* Overo nuova descrizione dello stato presente di tutti prencipati, e republiche d'Italia

... di Gregorio Leti ... Geneva, G. e P. de la Pietra, 1675-76. 4 v. Part I, pp. 43-72. DLC BM BN

32. Lucchesini, Giovanni Lorenzo. *Silvarum.* Roma, Tinassi, 1671. v. 1, p. 261-299.

33. Lupis, Antonio. *Amazzone scozzese.* Venetia, Ferretti, 1685. p. 5.

34. Lupis, Antonio. *L'Erovina veneta,* ovvero la vita di Elena Lucrezia Cornaro. Venetia, Curti, 1689. 133 p. p. 1-124 e riproduzione de la medaglia fatta coniare dall'Università, e ritratto di suor Isabella Piccini. BM

35. Macedo, Francisco de. *Lucerna Macedi ad lucernam cleanthis.* Padova, Frambotti, 1669.

36. Macedo, Francisco de. *Medulla historiae ecclesiasticae,* Patavii, Frambotti, 1671. 5 p. n. num.

37. Macedo, Francisco de. *Myrothecium morale.* Patavii, Cadorini, 1675. p. 184.

38. Macedo, Francisco de. *Panegirico sacro del serafico P.S. Francesco dedicato all'illustrissima signora Elena Lucrezia Cornara Piscopia.* Patavii, Cadorini, 1675. Dedica 1 p. n. num.

39. Macedo, Francisco de. *Panegyricus Dominae Helenae Corneliae,* Patavii, 1679.

40. Macedo, Francisco. *Picturae venetae urbis.* Venetiis, Cicras, 1670. p. 62.

41. Martial, Giovanni Battista. *Epos, parnassia apotheosis Helenae Lucretiae Corneliae Piscopiae.* Mediolani, Montin, 1686. pp. 1-15.

42. Muti, Giovanni Maria. *La Penna volante del Muti in certe lettere alla moda,* etc. Venetia, 1681. p. 157-158. BM

43. Muti, Giovanni Maria. *Le rotture del genio consacrato alla gran virtù della signora Patrona colendissima, la signora Elena Lucrezia*

Cornaro Piscopia. Venezia, Milocho, 1683. Preface 26 pp. n. num., and pp. 43-44, 63-65, 80, 202, 247.

44. Oliva, Giovanni Paolo. *Lettere.* Venezia, Baglioni, 1690. 2 vol. v. 1, p. 4, 144-147 V. 2, p. 7, 22, 41, 122, 173, 209-210, 219-220, 236-237, 263, 277-278.

45. Pacichelli, Giovanni Battista. *Memorie de'viaggi.* Napoli, Reg. Stampa, 1685. 3 vol. v. 3, p. 456.

46. Palazzi, Giovanni Canonico. *Aquila inter Lilia, sub qua Francorum Caesarun a Carolo Magno usque ad Conradum Imperatorem Occidentis* x . . . *Fasti exarantur.* Venetiis, Hertz, 1671. v. 1, p. 79-80. e ritratto del Langlois. BM BN

47. Perazzo, Joannes Benedictus. *Distichorum.* Venetiis, Poleti, 1684. p. 50, 134-135, 155.

48. Perazzo, Joannes Benedictus. *Opuscolo.* Venezia, Combi, 1668. p. 62-63.

49. Renaldini, Carol. *Commercium epistolicum.* Patavii, Frambotti, 1682. v. 3, p. 66-67, 81-91.

50. Renaldini, Carlo. *De resolutione et compositione mathematicae.* Patavii, Frambotti, 1668. 535 p. p. 157. BM BN

51. Renaldini, Carlo. *Geometra promotus,* Patavii, Frambotti, 1670. pars. II, p. 59.

52. Sansovini, Francesco. *Venetia, città nobilissima* . . . con aggiunta . . . da d. Giustiniano Martinioni. Venetia, Curti, 1663. libro 8, p. 374; libro 9, p. 389-391. DLC BM BN

53. Sonesio, Enrico. *Encomia urbis venetae,* Venetiis, Tinani, 1678. p. 91.

54. Vianoli, Alessandro Maria. *Historia veneta di Alessandro Maria Vianoli* . . . Venetia, G. G. Hertz 1680-84. 2 v. v. 2, p. 718. DLC BM BN

55. Vidali, Giovanni Battista. *Capricci serii delle Muse,* Venezia, 1677. p. 382-384.

56. Zopelli, Giacomo. *Trattenimenti poetici serii e geniali,* etc. Venetia, A. Bosio, 1676. p. 82-83. BM

B. *Printed Works—18th Century*

1. Alberti, Marcello. *Istoria delle donne scientiate.* Napoli, Mosca, 1740. CtY FU ICU BM

2. Applausi accademici alla laurea filosofica dell'illustrissima signora Elena Lucrezia Cornara Piscopia accademica Infeconda, composti e raccolti dall'Accademia stessa. *Journal des Scavans,* v. 13, 11 Sept., 1679. Paris, Witte, 1728. p. 145-146 e disegno di medaglione simbolico.

3. Armellini, Mariano. *Bibliotheca Benedictino-Casinensis,* . . . Assisii, Typis Feliciani & Philippi Campitelli Fratrum, 1731-32. 2 v. in 1. Part 1, p. 196-200. ICN MH MnCS BM BN

4. Bettinelli, Saverio. *Il Parnaso veneziano.* Venezia, Palese, 1796. 87 p. p. 33, 73, 76. NN IU NRU BM

5. Brandolese, Pietro. *Pitture, sculture, architetture, ed altre cose notabili di Padova.* Padova, P. Brandolese, 1795. p. 48, 238. DLC MiU CU CtY NcD PPULC BM BN

6. Camposampiero, Guglielmo. "Discorso accademico del 16 giugno 1723." *Discorsi accademici* di vari autori viventi intorno agli studi delle donne la maggior parte recitati nell'Accademia dei Ricoverati di Padova. Padova, Tip. Seminario, 1729. p. 8. DLC—under the title: Discorsi . . . BM—under Volpi, Giovanni Antonio. p. 8.

7. Cinelli Calvoli, Giovanni. *Biblioteca volante di Gio. Cinelli Cavoli,* continuata dal dottor Dionigi Andrea Sancassani. Ed 2. Venezia, Presso G. Albrizzi q. Girolamo, 1734-47. 4 v. v. 2, p. 194. DLC CtY NN MB MiU CLU MH WU DNLM NIC BM BN

8. *Dizionario storico-portatile di tutte le venete patrizie famiglie.* Venezia, Presso G. Bettinelli, 1780. 168 p. p. 56-57. DLC CtY PPL

9. Facciolati, Jacopo. *Fasti gymnasii patavini.* Patavii, Typis Seminarii, apud Joannem Manfre, 1757. 3 pts. in 1. Part 3, p. 237. NIC NNC MH KU-M NNNAM ICU DNLM ICN IU BM BN

10. Freschot, Casimir. *La nobilta' veneta,* o'sia tutte le famiglie patrizie con le figure de suoi scudi & arme; historia di D. Casimiro Freschot. 2 ed. In Venetia, Appresso Gip. Gabriel Herta, Con Licenza de'Superiori 1707-1722. p. 100, 147-150, 294-295, 300-302. DLC CtY BM BN

11. Gaetani, Piero Antonio, Conte. *Museum Mazzuchellianum.* Venetiis, Typis Antonii Zatta. 1763. v. 2, p. 140-141 e tav. 133. MB PPL BM BN

12. Gimma, Giacinto. *Idea della storia dell'Italia letterata,* coll'ordine cronologico dal suo principio sino all'ultimo secolo. Napoli, F. Mosca, 1723. 2 v. v. 2, p. 668-669. ICN IU NjP MB CtY MdBJ BM BN

13. Gozzi, Luisa (Bergalli) Gozzi, contessa. *Componimenti poetici delle più illustri rimatrici d'ogni secolo, raccolti da Luisa Bergalli* . . . Venezia, Antonio Mora, 1726. 2 parts in 1 vol. v. 2, p. 280-281. DFo PU ICN CtY BN

14. Guasco, Giovanni. *Storia letteraria.* Reggio, Vedrotti, 1711. 384 p. p. 353. CtY IU ICU ICN NIC BM

15. Lorenz, Christian Heinrich. *Analecta literaria ad Helenae Lucretiae Corneliae Piscopiae, liberalium artium magistrae, vitam, Christophoro* . . . Altenburgi, literis richteriis, 1772. 28 p. BN

16. Mabillon, Jean. *Museum italicum,* sev collectio veterum scriptorum ex bibliothecis italicis, eruta a.d. Johanne Mabillon & D. Michaele Germain . . . Lutetiae Parisiorum, apud Montalant, 1724. 2 v. v. 1, part 1, p. 34-35. DLC BM BN

17. Maria de Agnesis. "Oratio accademica, 18 augustus 1723." *Discorsi accademici* di vari autori viventi intorno agli studi delle donne la maggior parte recitati nell'Accademia dei Ricoverati di Padova. Padova, Tip. Seminario, 1729. p. 104 DLC—under: Discorsi . . . BM—under Volpi, Giovanni Antonio. p. 104.

18. Moreri, Louis. *Le grand dictionnaire historique.* Paris, 1744. v. 3, p. 490. DLC BM BN—all dif. ed.

19. Niceron, Jean Pierre. *Memoires pour servir à l'historie des hommes illustres dans la re'publique des lettres,* avec un catalogue raisonne' de leurs ouvrages . . . Paris, Briasson, 1729-45. 43 v. in 44. v. 19, p. 21-29 v. 20, p. 170-171. DLC BM BN

20. *Nouveau Dictionnaire Historique.* Caen, Le Roy, 1789. v. 3, p. 84-85. BM

21. *Nouveau Dictionnaire Historique Portatif.* Amsterdam, Rey, 1771. v. 1, p. 618. BM—dif. ed.

22. *Nuovo dizionario istorico.* Napoli, Morelli, 1791. v. 7, p. 338-389.

23. Papadopoulos, Nikolaos Komnenos. *Nicolai Comneni Papodopouli Historia Gymnasii Patavini,* Venetiis, Coleti. 1726. 2 vol. v. 2, p. 316. BM BN

24. Pentolini, F. G. *Le donne illustri: Poema.* Livorno, Falorni, 1776. v. 1, p. 155-156, canto II, stanza 58.

25. Relazione della famosissima laurea in filosofia dell'illustrissima et eccellentissima signora Elena Lucrezia Cornara in Padova 1678. *Journal des scavans,* v. 32, 12 Sept. 1678. Paris, Witte, 1724. p. 204.

26. Salomoni, Jacopo. *Inscriptiones patavinae, appendix urbis et agris.* Patavii, Corona, 1708. 311 p. p. 132. BM

27. Salomoni, Jacopo. *Urbis Patavinae inscriptiones sacrae et prophanae*

a magistro Jacobo Salomonio, . . . *collectae.*—Patavii, su mpt. J. B. Caesari, 1701. 632 p. p. 362, 434. BM BN

28. Savonarola, Raffaello. *Universus terrarum orbis scriptorum calamo delineatus.* Studio et labore Alphonsi Lasor a Varea, pseud. Patavii, Frambotti, 1713. v. 2, p. 345-346. DLC BM BN

29. Tiraboschi, Girolamo. *Biblioteca modenese.* Modena, Società Tipografica, 1781-1786. 6 vol. v. 3, p. 132. LC BM BN

30. Tiraboschi, Girolamo. *Storia della letteratura italiana.* Venezia, 1795-1796. 9 vol. in 16. v. 8, p. 441-442. LC BM BN

31. Verci, Giovanni Battista. *Notizie intorno alla vita e alle opere de'pittori, scultori e intagliatori della città di Bassano.* Venezia, G. Gatti, 1775. 328 p. p. 299-300. DLC BM BN

32. *Vitae selectae quorundam eruditissimorum ac illustrium Virorum, ut et Helenae Cornarae et Cassandrae Fidelis a clarissimis viris scriptae . . . in unum volumen redactae* (by C. Gryphius). Vratislaviae, Bauchius. 1711. p. 240-275. BM BN

B. *Printed Works—19th Century*

1. Abrantes, Laure Saint-Martin (Permon) Junot, Duchesse d'. *Vite e ritratti delle donne celebri.* Milano, Ubicini, 1839. v. 5, p. 221-234. MH BM

2. *American catholic quarterly review.* Philadelphia, 1876-1924. Oct. 1896.

3. *Analecta Bollandiana.* Bruxelles, 1898. v. 17, 1898, p. 354.

4. *Attività letteraria nel Monastero S. Benedecti de Urbe.* Roma, Vaticana, 1897. p. 4-6.

5. Bailey, Anna. "A daughter of the doges." *American catholic quarterly review.* Philadelphia, 1876-1924. v. 21, 1896, p. 820-827.

6. Battagia, Michele. *Delle accademie veneziane.* Venezia, Orlandelli, 1826. 134 p. p. 50-51. NNC NRU

[70]

7. Battagia, Michele. *Della nobiltà patrizia veneta; saggio storico.* Venezia, Alvisopoli, 1816. 68 p. p. 58. NRU IU BM

8. *Biografia universale antica e moderna.* Venezia, Alvisopoli, 1823. Translation of: Biographie universelle founded by J. F. Michaud and his brother L. G. Michaud. v. 13, p. 227. IU PPULC PU—dif. ed. BM

9. Camerini, Eugenio. *Donne illustri, biografie:* Milano, P. Carrara, 1878. 254 p. p. 179-183. CU—microfilm. BM

10. Canonici Fachini, Ginevra. *Prospetto biografico delle donne italiane rinomate in letteratura dal secolo decimoquarto sino a' giorni nostri* . . . Venezia, Alvisopoli, 1824. 274 p. p. 159. DLC IU CtY BM

11. Carrer, Luigi. *Anello di sette gemme; o, Venezia e la sua storia.* Venezia, Gondoliere. 1838. 734 pp. p. 697-716 e ritratto di Fanoli e Viviani. MB PPLT MH ICU PPULC NNC NcD NRU

12. *Catholic world.* A monthly magazine of general literature and science. New York, 1865-. February 1891.

13. Cicogna, Emmanuele Antonio. *Delle inscrizioni veneziane.* Venezia, G. Orlandelli, 1824-53. 6 v. v. 4, p. 378, 443. v. 5, p. 448. v. 6, p. 855. NRU CU NNC IU WU MH ICN BM BN

14. Cicogna, Emmanuele Antonio. *Saggio di bibliografia veneziana.* Venezia, Merlo, 1847. 942 p. p. 296, 315, 357, 365, 370, 404. DLC PPULC CU NIC BM BN

15. *Dizionario biografico nazionale.* Firenze, Passigli, 1842. v. 2 p. 475.

16. *Le donne illustri del regno lombardo-veneto.* Milano, Vallardi, 1828. p. 97-101.

17. *Le donne illustri d'Italia. Almanacco per l'anno 1827.* Milano, Ubicini, 1826. p. 82.

18. F.M.C. *Centuria di donne illustri italiane.* Milano, 1890. p. 471.

19. Federici, Fortunato. *Della biblioteca di S. Giustina di Padova.* Padova, Tip. Bettoni, 1815. 85 p. p. 71, n. 58. ICU BM BN

20. Feller, François Xavier de. *Dizionario storico.* Venezia, Tasso, 1832. v. 3, p. 673.

21. Ferraris, Carlo Francesco. *Elena Lucrezia Cornaro Piscopia e la sua tomba.* Padova, Randi, 1898. p. 129-133.

22. Ferri, Pietro Leopoldo, conte. *Biblioteca femminile Italiana.* Padova, Tipografia Crescini, 1842. 411 p. p. 130-131, 273, 275-276. DLC PPLT MH NNGr CLU MiU MB ICJ BM BN

23. Fontana, Giovanni Jacopo. *Cento palazzi fra i più celebri di Venezia.* Venezia, Naratovich, 1865. 445 p. p. 131-138. NRU NNC MH

24. Frati, Ludovico. *La Donna italiana secondo i più recenti studi.* Torino, Fratelli Bocca. 1899. p. 98. ICJ NN

25. Galleria (piccola) poetica di donne veneziane. *Strennetta per l'anno nuovo 1852.* Mestre, *1851.* p. 10-12.

26. Gamba, Bartolommeo. *Alcuni ritratti di donne illustri delle provincie veneziane.* Venezia, Tip. di Alvisopoli, 1826. p. 3, n. num. Misc. Fasc. 7 e ritratto No. 9 del Rosetti. DLC BM

27. Gamba, Bartolomeo, "Elena Cornar Piscopia." *La letteratura veneziana e le sue donne passate e presenti.* Venezia, Fiucco, 1864. p. 83, 105.

28. Giurato, Giuseppe. "Memorie venete in monumenti di Roma: Inscrizioni ad Elena Lucrezia Cornaro Piscopia." *Archivio veneto,* nuova serie. v. 27, 1884, p. 120-121.

29. Gonzati, Bernardo. *La basilica di S. Antonio di Padova.* Padova, A. Bianchi, 1852-53. 2 v. v. 2, p. 309-312. IU CU NIC DHN CtY MH NjP BM BN

30. Harmonville, A. L. d'. *Dizionario delle date . . .* Venezia, Antonelli, 1844. v. 2, p. 652. LC BM—both have dif. ed.

31. Hoefer, Johann Christian Ferdinand. *Nouvelle biographie géné-rale.* Paris, Firmin-Didot frères, 1852-1866. 46 vol. v. 11, p. 842. BM BN

32. Jose, Antonio Maria. *I codici manoscritti della biblioteca Antoniana di Padova.* Padova, Messaggero, 1886. p. 147. DLC—under Padua. Biblioteca Antoniana—dif. ed.

33. Ladvocat, Jean Baptiste. *Dizionario storico portatile.* Bassano, Remondini, 1824. v. 2, p. 139.

34. La letteratura veneziana e le sue dame passate e presenti. *Strenna Veneziana per il 1865.* Venezia, Tip .del 1862-. 1864, p. 83, 105-107, tav. 104.

35. Levati, Ambrogio. *Dizionario biografico cronologico diviso per classi degli uomini illustri* . . . Classe V: Donne illustri. Milano, Bettoni, 1821. 3 vol. v. 1, p. 159-160.

36. Morelli, Jacopo. *Della cultura della poesia presso li veneziani.* Venezia, Alvisopoli, 1820. v. 1, p. 223-224.

37. Musatti, Eugenio. *La Donna in Venezia.* Padova, Draghi, 1891. 270 p. p. 168-170. BM

38. Nani-Mocenigo, Filippo. *Della letteratura veneziana del secolo XIX* . . . Venezia, Emporio, 1891. 307 p. v. 1, p. 175. BM

39. Oettinger, Eduard Maria. *Bibliographie biographique universelle.* Paris, Klingksieck, 1850. 2 v. p. 132.

40. Prandi, Girolamo. *Elogio storico all'Abate Casinese Don Benedetto Bacchini,* etc. Bologna, 1814. p. 17. BM

41. Pynsent, Mathilde. *The life of Helen Lucretia Cornaro Piscopia,* oblate of the order of St. Benedict and doctor in the University of Padua. Rome, St. Benedict's, 1896. 128 p. DLC —this title is entered: Deza, Massimilliano and others.

42. R. W. "Helena Scholastica Cornara, eine Oblatin O.S.B."

St. Benedikts stimmen. Lambach; Prague, 1877-1915. v. 15, 1891, p. 269-275.

43. *Raccolta delle vere da pozzo in Venezia.* Venezia, Ongania, 1889. Part 1, n. 75, Part 2, n. 197.

44. Rebiere, Alphonse. *Les femmes dans la science.* Paris, Nony, 1897. 359 p. p. 79. DLC BM BN

45. *Revue bénédictine.* Abbaye de Maredsous. Belgium. 1884- v. 13, 1896, p. 325, v. 15, 1898, p. 548, v. 16, 1899, p. 177.

46. Rio, Alexis François. "Elena Cornaro ou la martyre de l'humilité." *Les quatres martyres.* Paris, Bray, 1856. p. 165. BM BN

47. Santa, G. Dalla. Review of the articles written by Angelo de Santi (see No. 48 of this bibliography). *Nuovo Archivio veneto, 1899.* v. 18, 1899, p. 238-239.

48. Santi, Angelo de. "Elena Lucrezia Cornaro Piscopia (1646-1684): Nuove ricerche." *Civilta cattolica.* Rome, 1850- Serie 17, 1898, v. 4, p. 172-186, 421-440, 678-689. Serie 17, v. 5, 1899, p. 176-193, 433-447. These articles are reviewed by G. Dalla Santa. *Nuovo Archivio Veneto,* v. 18, 1899, p. 238-239.

49. *Specilegium Benedictinum.* Roma, Monastero S. Benedetto, 1-4, 1896-1899.

50. Tassini, Giuseppe. *Alcuni palazzi ed antichi edifizi di Venezia,* Venezia, Fontana, 1879. 296 p. p. 60-65. DLC

51. Tettoni, Emma. "Le scienziate italiane." *La donna italiana: conferenze tenute all'eposizione Beatrice di Firenze.* Firenze, Civelli, 1890. p. 268, 273-274. DLC-P4 NIC

52. Tommaseo, Nicolo. *Dizionario estetico.* Milano, Bernardoni, 1852. 2 pt. p. 80. BM BN

53. Ungherini, Aglauro. *Manuel de bibliographie biographique et d'iconographie des femmes célèbres . . .* Turin, L. Roux & Viarenge; Paris, Nelsson, 1892. v. 1, p. 190. DLC BM BN

54. *Venezia e le sue lagune.* Venezia, Antonelli, 1847. 2 vol. in 3. v. 1, part. 2, p. 434; v. 2, part. 2, p. 420.

55. Verona, Agostino. *Le donne illustri d'Italia.* Milano, F. Colombo 1864. 110 p. DLC

B. *Printed Works—20th Century*

1. Americani al Po': Omaggio degli studenti alla prima laureata. *Avvenire d'Italia.* v. 71, 1966, no. 108, p. 6.

2. Barbiera, Raffaello. *Italiane gloriose: Medaglioni.* Milano, A. Vallardi, 1923. p. 251-257. MH

3. Belloni, Antonio. *Il seicento.* Milano, F. Vallardi, 1929. 606 p. (added t.-p.: Storia letteraria d'Italia, v. 7). BM MiU NN MH PU DLC

4. Blasi, Jolanda de. *Le scrittrici italiane dalle origini al 1800* (con 32 tavole fuori testo). Firenze, Casa editrice "Nemi", 1930. 407 p. p. 184-185. BM NN PULC CU TxU TU CtY MiU OCU NNC

5. Camerini, Eugenio. *Anima femminile.* Padova, n.d.

6. Casati, Giovanni. *Dizionario degli scrittori d'Italia* (dalle origini fino ai viventi) . . . Milano. R. Ghirlanda 1926. v. 2, p. 197, n. 1232. BM DLC CSt CtY MH NcD OCU MiU

7. Checchi, Marcello . *Padova, guida ai monumenti e alle opere d'arte.* Di Marcello Checchi, Luigi Gaudenzio e Lucio Grossato. Venezia, N. Pozza 1961. p. 120-121, 323, 325, 403. NIC MdU CU LNHT NcD ICU MiU NjP

8. Cimnaghi, R. M. "Visita a Elena." *La Fiera letteraria.* Milano, Roma, 1929- 1952, no. 36.

9. Cinti, Decio. *Dizionario degli scrittori italiani contemporanei.* Milano, Sonzogno, 1919. 200 p. Ncd WU—dif. ed.

10. Cornaro, Luigi. *The art of living long;* a new and improved English version of the treatise of the celebrated Venetian centenarian, Louis Cornaro, with essays by Joseph Addison, Lord Bacon, and Sir William Temple . . . Milwaukee, W. F. Butler, 1903. 214 p. p. 159-167, 171-173. BM BN DLC OrCS DNLM NN

11. Croce, Benedetto. "Appunti di letteratura secentesca inedita o rara." *La Critica;* rivista di letteratura, storia di filosofia. Napoli, Bari. v. 1-42, 1903-1944, s. 3, 1929, v. 27, fasc. 6, p. 471-472.

12. Dalmazzo, Fanny. *Lucrezia Cornaro Piscopia oblata benedettina.* Subiaco, 1943. p. 117.

13. *Delle donne illustri italiane dal sec. XIII al XIX secolo.* Roma, n.d. p. 210.

14. *Dizionario di cultura universale.* Pubblicato sotto la direzione di Leo Pollini. Milano, F. Vallardi 1907. 4 v. p. 447. IU—dif. ed.

15. *Enciclopedia biografica-bibliografica,* diretta da Francesco Orestano. Milano, E.B.B.I., 1940. s. 6, Poetesse e scrittrici. p. 175-176 e ritratto del Fanoli e Viviani. s. 7, italiane, eroine, ispiratrici, donne di eccezione, p. 110.

16. *Enciclopedia de la religión católica.* Barcelona, Dalmau y Jover, 1950- v. 2, p. 1135. DCM IMunS NIC CtY-D PLatS NN CLgA OrU DLC

17. *Enciclopedia ecclesiastica,* pubblicata sotto la direzione dell' eccellenza mons. Adriano Bernareggi . . . Milano, F. Vallardi; Torino, Pontificia Marietti, 1942—v. 2, 1944, p. 323. DLC NcU MH MH-AH

18. *Enciclopedia Italiana.* Roma, Treccani, 1931-1939. v. 9, p. 418-419.

19. *Enciclopedia Universale.* Milano, Rizzoli-Larousse, 1964. v. 4, p. 525.

20. *Enciclopedia Universale Illustrata.* Milano, Vallardi, 1933. v. 7, p. 16.

21. Fabris, Giovanni. *Gli scolari illustri dell'Università di Padova.* Padova, Stab. tip. L. Penada, 1941. 68 p. p. 44. NIC CtY NN

22. Favaro, Antonio. *L'Università di Padova.* Venezia, Ferrari, 1922. 22 p. p. 62. DCU MnU CtY-M RPB ICN NNC NcD MWelC NN

23. Favaro, Antonio. *L'Università di Padova;* di Antonio Favaro e Roberto Cessi. Padova, Zanocco, 1946. p. 122, 168.

24. Fedele, Pietro. *Grande dizionario enciclopedico.* Torino, Unione Tip. Torinese, 1931. v. 3, p. 673.

25. Ferraris, Carlo Francesco. *Cinque anni di rettorato nella R. Università di Padova, 1891-92 al 1895-96.* Roma, Stabilimento poligrafico 1922. 104 p. p. 99. CU NIC

26. François, Jean. *Bibliothèque générale des écrivains de l'Ordre de Saint Benoit,* Bouillon, 1777-1778. Louvain, Bibliothèque S. J., 1961. 4 v. Reproduction anastatique accompagnee d'une note liminaire sur les bibliographies bénédictines. p. 218. NjPT IUC MH-AH NjP ICN

27. Garollo, Gottardo. *Dizionario biografico universale.* Milano, U. Hoepli, 1907. 2 v. p. 578. BM BN DLC LU CU TxU PBm PP ODW OCU PU MH ICJ NN

28. *Grande Dizionario Enciclopedico.* Torino, U.T.E.T., 1955. p. 1103.

29. *Grande enciclopedia popolare Sonzogno;* pubblicata sotto la direzione di Palmiro Premoli . . . Milano, Sonzogno 1928— 22 v. v. 4, p. 722. NG 0381428 ICU NN

30. Grignola, G. *Guida artistica ai Santuari Antoniani di Padova.* Padova, 1930. 2220. p. 30. OrU

31. Kapsner, Oliver Leonard. *A Benedictine bibliography:* an author-subject union list. Compiled for the Library Science Section

of the American Benedictine Academy. With a foreword by Anselmo M. Cardinal Albareda. 2. ed. Collegeville, Minn., St. John's Abbey Press, 1962. 2 v. v. 2. BM CSt MoSW DCU CLU NjR CU

32. Larousse, Pierre. *Nouveau Larousse illustre;* dictionnaire universel encyclopédique, publié sous la direction de Claude Auge . . . Paris, Librairie Larousse, n.d. p. 283.

33. Marzolo, Vittoria Scimemi. "Elena Lucrezia Cornaro Piscopia". *Vita e Pensiero,* v. XI, 1925. p. 486-494.

34. Maylender, Michele. *Storia delle accademie d'Italia.* Bologna, L. Cappelli, 1926-30. v. 3, p. 256. v. 6, p. 196, 444. BM DLC

35. Molmenti, Pompeo Gherardo. *La storia di Venezia nella vita privata, dalle origini alla caduta della repubblica.* Bergamo, Istituto Italiano d'arti grafiche, 1912. 3 v. p. 421, 457. BM BN DLC

36. Mondrone, Domenico. "Da una gustosa curiosità storica al dottorato di S. Teresa d'Avila." *Civiltà Cattolica.* Rome. v. 121, 1970, p. 458-459.

37. Musatti, Eugenio. *Storia di Venezia.* Milano, Treves, 1936. v. 2, p. 231-232.

38. Nucci, Nelly. "Elena Lucrezia Cornaro Piscopia." *Patavina Libertas,* Treviso, Longo-Zoppelli, 1922. p. 20-21.

39. Occioni-Bonaffons, Giuseppe. "Brevi cenni sulle Accademie in Venezia." *Ateneo veneto nel suo primo centennio.* Venezia, Bortoli, 1912. p. 11.

40. Pace, E. A. "Cornaro Eleana Lucrezia." *The Catholic Encyclopedia.* N. Y., Hebermann, 1908. v. 4, p. 373.

41. Pepi, Ruperto. *L'Abbazia di Santa Giustina in Padova;* storia e arte. Padova, Edizioni Monaci Benedettini, 1966. 203 p. p. 111. DLC

42. La Prima Donna Laureata. *Il Gazzettino.* v. 80, 1966, No. 107, p. 5.

43. *Raccolta delle vere da pozzo in Venezia.* Venezia, Ongania, 1911. Tav. 177.

44. Redlich, V. "Cornaro Elena Lucrezia Piscopia." *Lexikon für Theologie und Kirche.* Freiburg, Herder, 1957- v. 3, 1959, p. 57. PPLas CSt NcD LU NNC CBPac CLU MiEM CtW

45. Rocco, Giuseppe. *I luoghi di San Gregorio;* strade e paesi nell'itinerario pastorale del vescovo Barbarigo. Padova, Tip. Antoniana, 1961. 334 p. p. 242-245. CLU BM BN

46. Rodocanachi, Emmanuel Pierre. . . . *La femme italienne avant, pendant et après la renaissance; sa vie privée et mondaine, son influence sociale.* Paris. Hachette, 1907. 439 p. p. 44. BM BN DLC—1922 ed.

47. Rotary Club di Padova. *Gli edifici di Alvise Cornaro a Padova.* Stedio, Aquila, 1970.

48. *Santo;* Rivista antoniana di Storia, dottrina, arte. (Centro Studi Antoniani) Padova. 1, 1961- v. 4, 1964, fasc. 1, p. 36, 40. fasc. 2, p. 193-194.

49. Serena, Sebastiano. *S. Gregorio Barbarigo e la vita spirituale e culturale nel suo Seminario di Padova;* lettere e saggi editi dagli amici in memoria. Padova, Editrice Antenore, 1963. 2 v. v. 1, p. 184-185, 215-216. NNC DCU NIC

50. Smith, P. D. "Cornaro Elena Lucrezia Piscopia." *New Catholic Encyclopedia.* New York, McGraw 1966. p. 332.

51. Spreti, Vittorio, marchese. *Enciclopedia storico-nobiliare italiana.* Milano, Carettoni, 1929. p. 541. DLC BM

52. Tassini, Giuseppe. *Curiosità veneziane.* Venezia, Fuga, 1915. p. 408-409. LC—1887 ed.

53. Ungherini, Aglauro. *Manuel de bibliographie, biographie et d'ico-nogrophie des femmes célèbris par un vieux bibliographile.* Supplement II, Turin, L. Roux, 1905 p. 358. DLC BM BN

54. *La Vie Bénédictine.* Abbaye Saint- Martin, Liguge (Vienna). 1935.

55. Vigodarzene, Luisa Cittadella. "Le grandi scolare." *L'Università di Padova nel VII centenario.* Numero unico. Padova, 15 maggio, 1922. p. 45-46.

56. Zanini, Lina. "Elena Cornaro Piscopia, prima laureata nell' Universita di Padova." *Viviamo,* rivista di attualità femminile. Catania, 1958-. v. 1., p. 61-64.

57. Zimmermann, Alfonso. *Kalendarium benedictinum.* Metten, 1934. V. 2, p. 498-499.

Bibliography of Printed Articles about the Cornaro Printed in the United States

1. A.A.U.W. *Journal,* American Association of University Women, November 1974, Gabrielle E. Forbush, "Elena Cornaro," pp. 30-32.

2. *Vassar Quarterly,* Vassar College, Spring 1973, Jane Howard Guernsey, "The Case of 'The Cornaro' A Vassar Mystery," pp. 27-29.

3. *Kappa Gamma Pi News,* Kappa Gamma Pi (National Catholic College Women's Honor Society) July 1974, Gabrielle E. Forbush, "Introducing Elena Lucrezia Cornaro Piscopia, 1646-1684," p. 4 & p. 8.

4. *Kappa Gamma Pi News,* Kappa Gamma Pi (National Catholic College Women's Honor Society) November 1974, Editorial by Frances Noetzel, "Cornaro, Patron Saint of Educated Women," p. 4.

5. *People,* National Council of Catholic Laity, June-July 1972, Gabrielle E. Forbush, "A Liberated Woman Circa 1678," pp. 14-15.

6. *Ms.* Magazine, January 1975, Gabrielle E. Forbush, "Lost Women," p. 56.

7. "Introducing Elena Lucrezia Cornaro Piscopia 1646-1684," Gabrielle E. Forbush, updated reprint of article in *People,* June-July 1972.

8. *Catholic Woman,* January-February 1975, Gabrielle E. Forbush, "A Woman for All Seasons," pp. 11-12.

Probably a likeness circa 1683-1684 when Elena Cornaro Piscopia was gravely ill.
(See next page for translation of inscriptions.)

Museo Civico—Padova

Translations in Baroque Frame

Elegiac Couplets Under Portrait—Elena Cornaro Piscopia, daughter of Giovanni Batista, a Noble, Chief Administrator.

This is distinguished virtue in a royal maiden.
Just as lofty Olympus glories in the Sun alone,
So the Earth boasts to rejoice in Elena alone.

Around inner edge of frame—Toil's reward recreates, honors, guides.

On book to right of portrait—She teaches.

Up on left column, down on right column—
What magnet is to iron, hence strength.
That the diamond rises preeminent in gold, hence brilliance.

That a stem has a crown, it [the stem] rises.
That a pillar is a column of distinction, forever.

Glossary

1. The Primacy

A Letter 1972

Università degli Studi di Padova
Istituto per la Storia
Dell'Università di Padova
35100 Padova, Nov. 21, 1972
Palazzo del Bo
Via 8 Febbraio, 9

Elena Cornaro Piscopia (born in Venice on June 5th, 1646 and deceased in Padua on July 26th, 1684) graduated in Philosophy at the University of Padua on June 25th, 1678. The old tradition, on the basis of which it was held that Cornaro was the first woman university graduate in the world, has now been confirmed definitely.

Between 1969 and 1972, this Institute addressed, to the 114 Universities in the world which were founded before the middle of the seventeenth century, a circular letter asking for rigorous documented information on their first woman graduate. The results of this laborious inquiry and of collateral historical research conducted by this Institute will be published in the next volume of *Quaderni per la Storia dell'Università di Padova* [periodical of the history of the University of Padua].

[85]

Henceforth, however, we can confirm that Elena Cornaro
Piscopia is the first woman graduate in the world.

The President
Institute for the History of the University of Padua
s/Prof. Paolo Sambin

Introductory statement

to *Estratto da Quaderni per la Storia dell'Università di Padova*, Padova 1974

ELENA LUCREZIA CORNARO PISCOPIA (1646-1684)
PRIMA DONNA LAUREATA

Il dottorato in filosofia conseguito a Padova il 25 giugno 1678 dalla veneziana Elena Lucrezia Cornaro Piscopia, è il primo dottorato—in tutto il mondo—conferito a una donna.

Comitati italiani e stranieri stanno già eleborando il programma per degnamente celebrare il terzo centenario, fra i molti forse fuori serie, di questa secentesca laurea padovana.

E imminente la pubblicazione di un profilo divulgativo di Elena Lucrezia Cornaro Piscopia tracciato da Nicola Fusco e pubblicato a cura dell' Università di Pittsburgh in Pennsylvania (USA). Inoltre Ludovico Maschietto sta preparando una biografia della stessa Cornaro condotta con rigore scientifico su nuovi documenti.

Intanto il prospetto che segue, presentando i risultati di una rigorosa indagine basata su documenti storici e svolta a raggio mondiale presso più di cento università,[1] ne dimostra e conferma il primato.[2]

MARIA TONZIG

1. Delle 114 sedi universitarie (ovviamente escluse quelle fondate dopo il 1678) interpellate dall'Istituto per la storia dell'Università di Padova non hanno risposto le seguenti: Bogotà (Nazion.), Cairo, Cuzco, Fes, Greifswald, Halle-Wittemberg, Istanbul, Leipzig, Lima, Limoges, Lisboa, Merida, Oviedo, Perugia, Quito, Sucre, Uxrainskaja. Hanno invece motivato la loro risposta negativa le Università di Edimburgo e Olomouc (entrambe non aperte alle donne), Napoli (l'archivio della quale fu distrutto dalla guerra), Mainz (attiva solo dal 1946), Valencia (la cui prima laureata è di data recente).

2. Malgrado accurate ricerche non si è riusciti a reperire documenti atti a comprovare la tuttora dubbia e più volte contestata notizia del dottorato in diritto che sarebbe stato conseguito presso l'Università di Bologna da Bitisia Gozzadini il 3 giugno 1236.

2. The Name Piscopia
Origin and Use by the Cornaro Family.

From *The Life of Helen Lucretia Cornaro Piscopia,* by Abbess Matilde Pynsent, 1896, pp. 9, 10.

"The palace where Helen Lucretia (1646-1684) first saw the light is one of the grandest in Venice, and is now known by the name of Loredano, as in 1703 Catherine Cornaro a grand-daughter of John Baptist married a Loredano and inherited her own family palace. It was built nine centuries ago, and is a harmony of Gothic and Byzantine architecture. The capitals of the pillars of the upper storey can merit no further need of praise than to say that they are like those of the exquisite church of St. Vitale of Ravenna which was formerly Benedictine. The Palace of the Cornaro is decorated in its interior with the rarest oriental marbles and sculpture; and the vestibule is a triumph of magnificence, with its five arches rising from four columns of Greek marble, capped by Byzantine capitals.

"Noble guests had been welcomed within its spacious walls, and to one of them was due certain heraldic arms adorning the front of the palace and the second name of Piscopia. When Peter Lusignan, King of Cyprus was on his way to the court of Innocent VI at Avignon, he and his retinue were received with royal welcome and honour by the famous Frederic Cornaro from 1363 to 1366. He not only entertained them with great magnificence but also furnished his royal guest with a loan of 60,000 gold ducats, as he had set out on his journey ill-provided with money. In his gratitude Peter bestowed on his host his Royal Arms, which were engraved upon the palace, and he also declared that he and his heirs should henceforth be Knights of the order instituted by Guy, his predecessor. Upon returning home he found himself unable to discharge his debt; so to make up for this in some way he presented to the Cornaro the palace and lands of Piscopia in

Cyprus, and from this the family derived its second name.

RCM Clarification:

Pynsent uses the urban term "palace" for the Cyprus home, whereas Fusco uses the more accurate term *"castle"* for the Cyprus rural inheritance.

There have been many Catherines in the Cornaro family, the best known being Catherine Queen of Cypress (fifteenth century). After the death of her husband King James and of their infant son, she gave the Crown of Cypress to the Doge of Venice. This historic event is the theme of a German opera by Franz Lochner, translated into French and English. Interestingly, it is also the subject of a large stained glass window in the old Phipps Mansion, now the home of Arthur E. Braun in Pittsburgh, Pennsylvania.

The Catherine buried in Saint Anthony lived in the seventeenth century, dying ten years before Elena Lucretia. However, this connection of the Cornaro family with the basilica of Saint Anthony in the seventeenth century probably explains why parents of our Cornaro wished to have her buried there and ordered the magnificent sarcophagus which was never occupied, and does not now remain.

3. Official Records, Sacred College, Padua June 24, 25, 1678

Translations from the "Official Records of the Sacred College of Philosophers and Physicians," Padua, Friday, June 24, and Saturday, June 25, 1678.

Editor's Note: In 1932, the late Professor Evan Sage, then chairman of the Department of Classics, University of Pittsburgh, translated the Records of June 25. In 1975, Emeritus Professor Arthur Young, a successor and now a retired chairman of the same department, translated the records of both June 24 and June 25. Professor Dennis C. McElrath, Director Centro Studi University of California in Padua, and Professor Lucia Rossetti, Archivist University of Padua, edited Dr. Sage's translation and made some minor changes. The scholars' translations agree in substance, differing only occasionally in individual choice of English words or phrases. Also, the accepted English punctuation in the translation makes easier reading.

Die sabbati 25 mens Junij 1678

Convocato Sacro Collegio pro examine in Philosoph.
...ma Elena Lucretia Cornelia Piscopia, ob multitudi-
ne generali locus solita angustiam necesse fuit
adire Cathedralem Ecclesiam, et in Sacello Beatiss.

. . . . .

Virginis Mariae denuo convocato Collegio coram
...re Excellmo Civitatis Rectoribus Hieronymo Basa-
dona Pretore, Aloysio Mocenico Prefecto ...mo Vice
Alexandro Mantuano, et generosissimo Vice Sindico,
ubi interfuere infrascripti Nobiles, et Excell Patres
videlicet &

. . . . .

Examen et appro-
batio in Theol
more Nob:
...me et exc...ma d.
Elene Lucretia
Cornelie Piscopie
H. V.

Et in predicto Sacello pleno Collegio iamscripta ...ma
Elena Lucretia Cornelia Piscopia recitavit in
Philosophia more Nobilium, duo Puncta heri mane
illi sorte assignata; in quorum explicatione tam egregie
ac excellenter se gessit, ut absoluto eiusdem Nobilis
Virginis examine, raro et admirabili exemplo fue-
runt de more suffragationes urnaque delata ad
Nobil et Excell d. Jo: Dominico de Tesariis ut Priore
ceterosque de Banca suffragationis gratia peragente
Cum autem omnes Collegij doctores alta voce pronun-
ciaverint tam sublimem Punctorum recitationem Nobil
ori forma, quam per suffragia subijcienda esse
propterea hoc audito ...ma predicta, reiteratis
vocibus reverenter tamen, instetit ut iuxta
consuetudinem ad secreta omnino suffraga-

Portions of Records of the Sacred College, 25 June 1678.

nones deueniretur; sed in eam opinionem abierunt
ut honestum ac decens arbitrarentur examen. Propterea
Ill.mus D.nus Io: Domin.s de Tessarijs V.e Prior insurrexit
dicens, quamuis dispositio statutorum decernat, ut examen secretæ suffragatione exponatur, quia nihilominus
hæc Heroina, tam excellenter, tamq. excelse se gessit
petat ob id suffragatione prætermissa insuetum modum
explorandi mentes secreto Patres adhibere, unde propo-
suit ipsis, ac uniuerso Collegio, num comunis accla-
matio placeret, et omnes uno ore responderunt placet,
atq. hunc in modum comuni consensu acclamatione
et uiue uocis oraculo Ill.ma et Exc.na Helena Lucretia Cornelia prædicta Philosophiæ Magistra et Doctrix
acclamata fuit coram uniuerso doctorum cœtu maxi-
ma Nobilium populiq. Frequentia; mox accessit
prædicta Nobilis Virgo ut prius more solito rea-
ssisset, ad lauream doctoralem suscipiendam quas
relectas, ornatasq. uerbis petijt ab Ill.mo D.no Carolo
Renaldino Promotore suo Patrino Anconitano Poemi
III In Ducis eiusq. Philosopho ac Mathematico et
hac Celeberrima Academia Patauina Philosopho primæ
Sedis; qui statim secretexit et cœtas omnes suptadictis
ornata et erudita quidem Oratione Nobilitatem atq.
uirtutes Heroinæ prædictæ comendauit summo
cum audientum plausu, atq. tandem Coronas ex
Lauro tempora ipsius redimiuit, libros eidem
exibuit, digito annulum inseruit, et Epinicion Pelli-
ceum humeris eiusdem induit
Et dissolutum Collegium

Friday, June 24, 1678

Their Honorable Excellencies convened were Angelus Montagnana, Prior; Antonious de Musattus, Provincial; Petrus Saviolus, Syndic.

The theses stated below were drawn by lot, in the tradition of the Nobles, for the examination in philosophy of the Very Illustrious Elena Lucretia Cornelia Piscopia, noble maiden: From the thesis of the *Posteriora,* text 90 "Si igitur scire ut poscimus, etc." From the thesis of the *Physica,* text 42 "Quod igitur contraria quodadmodum."

[Editor Note: The theses which the Cornaro was to expound were selected *by lot.* She was unaware of these selections until she appeared on the following day before "the full College" to discuss and defend them.]

Saturday, June 25, 1678

When the Sacred College was convened for the purpose of examining in Philosophy the Very Illustrious Elena Lucretia Cornelia Piscopia, by reason of the large attendance and the cramped quarters of the usual meeting place it was necessary to repair to the Cathedral and to reconvene the College in the sanctuary of the Most Blessed Virgin Mary in the presence of the Most Illustrious and Excellent Governors of the City: Hieronymus Hasadona, Praetor, Aloysius Mocenicus, prefect, the Very Reverend Vicar Alexander of Mantua, and the Very Honorable Vice-syndic. There were present the following Nobles and Distinguished Fathers, namely: Sponsors—Hieronymus Frizimelica, Count and Knight of Rubert, Carolus Renaldinus, Angelus Montagnana, Ermegildus Pera.

On One Side	On the Other
Io. Petrus Saviolus, syndic	Georgius a Turre
Io. Dominicus de Tessariis, Vice-prior	Sebastianus Scarabitius
	Palmerinus Ianua
Ludovicus Saxonia	Nicolaus Campilongus

Ermegildus Pera
Count Petrus Franzanus
Vincentius Anselmus
Franciscus Bosellus
Prosper Thedeschi
Io. Pompilius Scotto
Hercules Saxonia
Franciscus Zacco, nobleman
Hieronymus Vergerius
Iacobus Cadenedus
Aloysius Speronus
Hieronymus Captivatius, senior
Iacobus Bonzaninus
Count Alexander Borromaeus
Hillarius Spinelli
Dominicus de Marchetis
Ioannes Cicalla
Albanius Albanensis
Alexander Mussatus
Antonius de Marchettis
Aldrigettus Aldrighetti
Io. Antonius Perotius
Ioannes Capilisteus
Alverius Zacco
Marcus Antonius Franchinus
Severinus Bellini
Antonius Mazonus
Horatius Brentus
Ioanne Ursatus

Marsilius Papafava
Iulius Massatus
Iacobus Trentus
Franciscus Bonbardenus
Antonius Maria Ursatus, Knight
Carolus Patinus
Nicolaus Frascata
Vincentius Pasqualigo, nobleman
Hieronymus Bradiolus
Io. Baptista Bradiolus
Count Franciscus Silvatious
Count Bartholomaeus Silvatious,
    canon
Prosdocimus Bosellus
Marcus Antonius Mussatus
Alexander Vigontia
Hieronymus Captivatius, junior
Alexander Bellafinus
Io. Augustus Scotus
Io. Franciscus Frangina
Carolus Mussatus
Io. Christopherus Massimus
Sulimanus Bradiolus
Tissus Bellafinus
Count Nicolaus Tebaldi
Angelus Casale
Marcus Antonius Peregrinus
Io. Vincentius Albanensis
Nanius Falaguasta

And in the aforesaid sanctuary, before the full College, the aforementioned Most Illustrious Elena Lucretia Cornelia Piscopia in the tradition of the Nobles discoursed in Philosophy on the two theses assigned to her by lot yesterday morning, and in the defense of them she conducted herself with such outstanding merit that when the examination of the same young lady was finished and her achievement considered commendable, the voting urns were brought down in accordance with the voting procedure to His Excellence the noble

Io. Dominicus de Tessariis, Vice-Prior, and the others, assembled at the Bench for the vote.

All the Doctors of the College proclaimed clearly that so splendid an exposition of the Theses should be rewarded more conspicuously than by submission to a ballot. The illustrious young woman repeatedly but humbly begged a secret ballot, according to the customary procedure. Thereupon the very honorable Vice-Prior Johannes Dominius de Tessariis arose and said that although the statutes decreed that examination be subject to secret ballot, nevertheless this remarkable girl had conducted herself with such excellence and distinction it would be proper for the Fathers to omit the secret ballot and employ an extraordinary procedure. Wherefore, he asked them and the whole College for an opinion as to whether an unanimous acclamation was their pleasure. All responded unanimously in the affirmative. And in this way, by common consent and viva voce the very illustrious and most exalted Helena Lucretia Cornelia Piscopia was acclaimed Master and Doctor of Philosophy in the presence of the entire assemblage of Doctors and the very large gathering of nobles and people. Soon the noble maiden, who earlier had withdrawn according to custom, approached and with well chosen, elegant words sought the doctoral Laurel from the very illustrious Master Carolus Renaldinus, her sponsor, a patrician from Ancona, Philosopher and Mathematician "primae sedis" to Cosimi III, Duke of Etruria, and mathematician and philosopher at the very celebrated Institution of Padua. He at once arose, and in the presence of all the company, with a polished and very learned address complimented the superiority and excellence of the aforesaid "heroine" amid the great applause of the audience. And finally he adorned her brows with the Laurel Crown, presented to her the proper books, placed the Ring on her finger, and put on her shoulders the Ermine Cape. The College then adjourned.

4. Three Books to Celebrate Tercentenary, 1978

As part of the 1978 Tercentenary to celebrate the graduation of the first woman in the world to receive a doctoral degree in philosophy, there will be three books—two in Padua, this one in Pittsburgh, Pennsylvania.

In Padua there will be published an Italian version of Monsignor Fusco's *Profile* and a scholarly biography by the Benedictine Ludovico Maschietto.

Dr. Maria Tonzig (January 1975) has described the scholarly Paduan volume thus: "A Benedictine monk, Ludovico Maschietto, is writing, according to a strict historic-cultural-literary method, a fresh biography accompanied by hitherto unpublished documents, the writings of Cornaro, and by a comprehensive bibliography."

Elena Lucrezia Cornaro Piscopia 1646-1684, the Pittsburgh book, has five parts: *Foreword* by Alfred M. Hunt, Trustee, The Hunt Foundation; *Introduction* by Ruth Crawford Mitchell, Director Emeritus, Nationality Rooms and Cultural Exchange Programs, University of Pittsburgh; *Profile* by the late Monsignor Nicola Fusco, P.A., Pastor of Mount Saint Peter Church, New Kensington, Pennsylvania; *Bibliography* by Maria Tonzig, eminent Scholar of Padua, Secretary General of Executive Committee and Honorary Committee, Padua; *Glossary* by Agnes Lynch Starrett, Emeritus Professor (English, The Humanities) and Emeritus Director-Editor, University of Pittsburgh Press.

5. The Profile

From the letter of the late Rt. Rev. Monsignor Nicola Fusco, P.A. to Mrs. Ruth Crawford Mitchell, October 12, 1971, written shortly before his death. (See *Introduction* p 17)

"*Remember that I never intended to produce a critical monograph of the Cornaro lady . . . loaded with all sorts of documentation. Mine is merely a Profile, that is, a short story. . . . I have never lost sight of the professional [attitude] of the Patavine University . . . where perhaps someone may become curious enough to make further researches and enable us to learn more about our Elena Piscopia. . . . I would like to see this humble opuscule of mine published. . . .*

"*St. Justina must have some money to move ahead with the work of St. Luke's Chapel, where Elena Cornaro should recover her eternal rest. . . .*

"*With best wishes and benediction.*"

s/Nicola Fusco

Editor's Note: Monsignor's letter indicates that he hoped his published *Profile* would help raise money to restore Elena Cornaro Piscopia's grave in Saint Luke's Chapel.

6. Illustrations

THE MEDAL (stamped in gold on Venetian-red book binding) Executed 1685, Francesco Neidin, sculptor.

Ordered struck by Sacred College of Philosophers and Physicians, University of Padua, by Laudatory Decree, January 11, 1685, six months after her death, to honor Elena Lucrezia Cornaro Piscopia—illustrious Magistra et Doctrix, first woman graduate of Padua—"singular event in the history of the University." Now in Bottacin Museum, annexed to Civic Museum (inv. Pad. n. 127). First published in print in Venice in 1689 and later, rarely. (See *Translation* p 96)

[95]

Translation Medal

Front: Helena Lucretia Cornelia Piscopia—Daughter of Joannis Battista, Noble High Magistrate, Laurel-crowned in Philosophy at Padua in the Year 1678.
John Francis Neidinger

Back: Not Without Reward
  By Decree of the College of Philosophy of Padua.

Symbolism: God's gifts fall gently on the earth and return to God   i.e., God's gifts to Elena Cornaro Piscopia:
her learning and piety.

Editor's Notes: The artist's name is spelled two ways, *Neidin* in Italian as it is in the records of the Bottacin Museum, and *Neidinger,* a Germanic spelling as it appears on the rim of the Medal.

This reproduction made from a drawing of the late Norton Peterson of Pittsburgh is used with permission of the Paduan Museum.

The Great Window, Vassar College Library, p. 10.
  Donor: Mrs. Frederick Ferris Thompson
  Architect: Francis Richmond Allen
  Studio Craftsmen: Church Glass & Decorating Company,
                U.S.A.
                Messrs. John Hardman & Company,
                Birmingham, England.

This beautiful stained glass window, installed in the Vassar Library (1906), was the gift of Mrs. Frederick Ferris Thompson to Vassar College. Working together on the designing and execution were the library building architect, Francis Richmond Allen, the Church Glass & Decorating Company of New York (Caryl Coleman, President), and Messrs. John Hardman & Company, Birmingham, England. Correspondence of September and November 1904 reveals that Mr. Coleman sent Mr. Hardman a tracing of the architectural structure of the window measured to scale, a brief summary of the life of The Cornaro, the scene to be represented, and suggestions for researching background information (photo of statue of Elena Piscopia and Benedictine Abbess Mathilda Pynsent's *Life of . . . Piscopia, 1896*). The Church Glass & Decorating Company also published a brochure: a brief life of Piscopia and an account of the conferring of the Doctorate, illustrated with the original sketch and the center and side panels from the window.

The design for the stained glass, a Renaissance concept of people, costumes, and color, was the work of Dunstan Powell, a partner in the English firm. Mr. Powell was a descendant of a long line of craftsmen which included Welby Pugin, architect for the interior of the English Houses of Parliament.

The window is a delightful artistic presentation of Elena Cornaro Piscopia's graduation scene. Color, composition, and detail, human and symbolic, exemplify the meaning of stained glass in an academic setting—the teaching value as well as the aesthetic.

The scene, the Lady Chapel of the Cathedral, is identified by the statue of the Holy Virgin—in the upper part of the center light.

The tracery shows a tree of knowledge whose branches bear varied flowers and fruits, among which are allegorical female figures representing the liberal arts—languages, mathematics, music, art, literature. Of them all Elena Piscopia was Master (Magistra).

The scholar stands before a throne-like chair elevated above those present at her graduation: University authorities, professors of all Paduan faculties, students, Venetian senators, invited dignitaries from Bologna, Ferrara, Perugia, Rome, and Naples. Her admiring father stands left as viewed. Further on, the University archivist waits to record her name and merits in the Paduan annals, and Professor Renaldi holds the laurel wreath. Outside the circle behind her on both sides are the public, "all sorts and conditions of people."

Before them all "the Cornaro" spoke for an hour in classic Latin, expounding difficult passages from Aristotle and responding to the challenging questions of scholars.

7. The Funeral Book of the Infecondi

LE POMPE FUNEBRI—Celebrate dá Signori Accademici Infecondi di Roma—per la Morte dell' Illustrissima Signora ELENA LUCREZIA CORNARA PISCOPIA Accademica detta L'Inalterabile—Dedicate alla Sereniss Republica di VENEZIA. In Padova, per il Cadorina, *Con lic. dé Sup.* MDCLXXXVI.

Memorial Ceremonies sponsored by the Infecondi Gentlemen Scholars of Rome—commemorating the death of their Most Illustrious Lady Scholar Elena Lucrezia Cornaro Piscopia, called the Inalterable—dedicated to the Most Serene Republic of Venice. Published in Padua by Cadorino, *duly authorized,* 1686.

Editorial Summary: Text and pictures feature the elaborate decorations in the College of the Barnabite Fathers—"with such sumptuous apparatus as was never seen before in the Academies of Rome." The Cornaro-Piscopia shield, in quarters and entire, was displayed prominently throughout the Hall of the College along with symbols of humane learning, both classic and medieval—all in most lavish baroque—cherubs, garlands, seascapes and landscapes, gold, precious and semiprecious gems, jasper columns, somber silk and velvet draperies, and flowery tributes to the Lady for her ancient lineage and her extraordinary learning. Speeches and sonnets adorn the text of the volume with praise extolling her scholarship and piety.

This book was one among Memorials issued at her death

by other learned societies. They are listed in the Bibliography. All are rare collectors' items. A copy of *Le Pompe Funebri* has been presented by the Class of 1912 to Vassar College. It shows that scholarship was recognized as a universal attribute by the Church, the State, and "gentlemen scholars," even three hundred years ago. But Elena Piscopia's academic degree was the "first in all the world" for womanhood.

8. Condensed Chronicle of Saint Luke's Chapel

The long history of Saint Luke's Chapel, linked with the history of Saint Justina, is highlighted by dramatic events through more than 600 years. Through fire, plague, theft, wars, and civil disturbances, through architectural construction and reconstruction (which goes on even as we write) the venerable little Chapel has remained steadfastly a Paduan treasure of art and holiness. For half its history, for nearly 300 years, it has held entombed among the graves of Benedictine abbots and monks the earthly remains of Elena Lucrezia Cornaro Piscopia, first woman academic laureate in the world. Her burial in this Chapel, which she so earnestly desired, has made it for the women of the world a shrine to Learning. Certainly, this book in which devoted men and women tell the story of "The Cornaro" should recount, however briefly, her beloved Chapel's history.

Most of the following details are garnered and condensed from paragraphs and notes transmitted to Pittsburgh from Dr. Maria Tonzig of Padua and translated by Dr. Francesca Colecchia of Duquesne University in Pittsburgh. Those concerning the Napoleonic Era are from *L'Abbazia di Santa Guistina in Padova* by Don Ruperti Pepi. (Edizone Monaci Benedictini. Stampe Poligrafica Modzina Luglio. Padova 1966.) He is the same Father Pepi, historian of the Benedictine Community in

Padua, who is in the photograph on p 15 of this book. The translation used was made by Father Ildephonse Wortman, O.S.B., Saint Vincent College, Latrobe, Pennsylvania.

The Chapel was built in the Fourteenth Century (1301-1316) to house the body of Saint Luke, brought from Constantinople, according to tradition circa Fifth or Sixth Centuries and buried in the Abbey. It was set parallel to the east-west axis of Saint Justina, the Benedictine Abbey Church (then a Romanesque basilica), and beside the bell tower and the Chapel of Saint Sigismondo.

It is difficult to show in photographs the outside of the Saint Luke Chapel itself. It is only a tiny part of the Saint Justina complex and it nestles very close to Saint Justina where rests the relic of the Saint for which the Chapel was named.

In 1436 Saint Luke's was decorated by Giovanni Storlato with frescoes representing the Saint's life. In 1453 Andrea Montegna painted panels for the Chapel. In 1457 Montegna also painted a large wooden altarpiece with Saint Luke in the center surrounded by the favorite saints of the abbot, the patron who commissioned the work.

In the middle of the Sixteenth Century it was decided to build a new basilica for Saint Justina in all the magnificence of the Renaissance style. On March 12, 1562, a grand procession celebrated the placing of the relics of the saints in the completed basilica. Saint Luke's body in a sarcophagus of green porphyry was moved to the apse of the left wing of Saint Justina where it is today.

Bereft of its treasure (Saint Luke's body) the Chapel no longer was venerated. In 1589 the need of a new burial place for the monks led the abbot to decide to convert "old Saint Luke's Chapel" into a "Chapel for the Dead." Because the new Renaissance basilica was on a higher level, the floor of Saint Luke's Chapel had to be raised more than seven feet. The space between the old floor and the new was filled with earth.

[100]

In the Mortuary of the Chapel, where she often knelt in prayer, Elena Lucrezia Cornaro Piscopia was buried in 1684, before the altar on the Epistle side.

It is thought that the inevitable dampness of the mortuary earth began the deterioration of the frescoes. In the 1700s when Padua was stricken with plague, the city fathers ordered all places where people gathered (libraries, chapels, cemeteries) to be covered with lime, and Saint Luke's Chapel again suffered damage to frescoes on walls and ceiling.

During the Napoleonic conquests in the late 1700s and early 1800s, the time of Napoleon's so-called Cisalpine Republic, the Benedictine treasures of Saint Justina Monastery and of the basilica and the chapels were dispersed among art galleries, museums, and some private collections. The Saint Luke altarpiece by Montegna was taken to its present location in Milan. In 1806 and 1807, most of the valuable Benedictine library was sent to Paris.

In 1810 the monks were dispersed, the last abbot fled to Avignon and later died there, and the State took possession of Saint Justina. In 1816 the books were scattered in various libraries and scientific institutes in Venice, in Padua, and in State Archives.

During the Nineteenth Century Italy became a favorite winter resort of the British. A Benedictine monastery for English-speaking nuns was established in Rome. The Abbess Mathilda Pynsent became interested in the Seventeenth and Eighteenth Century writings of Italian scholars [listed in the bibliography] about the Cornaro and wrote her biography in English. Further, she obtained permission from the Pope to go to Padua and have the grave in Saint Luke's Chapel opened to authenticate the existence of this unusual Seventeenth Century woman—a Benedictine oblate of the third degree. The story of this visit is told in her book, published in 1896, which is listed in the Bibliography [*Glossary* (pp 87, 101, 104)].

From 1915-1918, during World War I, the Benedictine complex of monastery, church, and chapels was used as a military barracks and warehouse. In 1919 the monks were allowed to return to their monastery, but only as custodians of a national monument. The Abbey was reconstructed, but placed under the administration of the neighboring Abbey of Praglia, Finalpia. (From *L'Abbazia di Santa Guistina* ... by Father Ruperti Pepi.)

By 1925 the monks had persuaded the Italian government to start restoring the Storlato frescoes, but the work was not completed. In 1942 the monastery of Saint Justina had its own Community reinstated. On January 23, 1943, after 123 years of interruptions, the Community elected a new abbot and activity within the monastery became vital once again.

Twentieth Century New World American interest in aiding the work on the Cornaro gravesite is explained in the Introduction to this book.

By 1969 the Institute of History at the University of Padua became involved, the director having pointed out that the claim of Primacy should not rest on tradition—there must be documentary evidence (*Glossary* p 85). Abbot Don Innocenzo DeAngelis then invited representatives of the University of Pittsburgh to meet in Padua with those concerned. Pledges were given to make every effort on both sides of the Atlantic to be ready in Padua in 1978 for visitors assembled from all over the world to celebrate the Tercentenary of the graduation of Elena Cornaro Piscopia.

This undertaking has been fraught with difficulties—continued changes of government in Italy; inflation in lire and dollars; deflation in dollar exchange; need to translate both ways' correspondence, research, and promotion material. But the committees in Padua are now forging ahead under the vigorous leadership of Co-presidents Don Innocenzo Negrato, O.S.B., the young Abbot of the Community of Saint Justina, Professor Aldo Stella of the Institute for Medieval and Modern

History (faculty of Letters and Philosophy) at the University of Padua, and with Dr. Maria Tonzig as Secretary General.

Today, in 1975, this American volume appears through the generosity of The Hunt Foundation of Pittsburgh and the ceaseless and persistent work for five years of a group of devoted American women who have volunteered their services in tribute to Elena Lucrezia Cornaro Piscopia.

This volume will be placed as a gift in reference libraries of American colleges, universities, and municipalities. In addition, the story told here has stimulated an American contribution to the Cornaro Restoration Fund. The Fund will be used specifically for the restoration of the Cornaro gravesite and the reinterment of the coffin in consecrated soil beneath a classical replica of the original black marble slab, incised with the Twentieth Century historically documented title, "Prima Donna Laureata Nel Mondo."

It is hoped that the newly established Ministry of Fine Arts will recognize the work of the "Comitato Per Le Celebrazioni Centenarie Di Elena Lucrezia Cornaro Piscopia" by completing restoration of the frescoes in the Fourteenth Century Gothic Chapel of Saint Luke. Meantime, the Italian government has officially renamed the venerable Chapel of Saint Luke, "Capella Cornaro."

9. Inscriptions on Gravestones and Statues

The Original 1684 Gravestone in Saint Luke Chapel

(See text pp 13, 14, 16)
(Translations by Brother Ildephonse OSB at
request of Archabbot Egbert Donovan of
Saint Vincent Archabbey, Latrobe, Pennsylvania)

Datur Omnibus Mori
—For Elena Lucrezia Cornaro Piscopia—

Daughter of John Baptist, Procurator of San Marco;
Surpassed Her Sex in Virtue and Learning;

Famous in the Memory of Posterity for her Doctoral Degree;

After Pronouncing Private Vows before Cornelius Cordanino,

Abbott of San Giorgio Maggiori, Early in Life Became an
Oblate of Saint Benedict, Persevering Therein Religiously;
At Her Own Request Was Buried in the Monastic Mortuary
After Intense Suffering.

—The Monks Piously Constructed This Tomb—
In the Year of Our Lord 1684

Second Grave Marker 1895

(The Abbess Matilda Pynsent)

In 1895 the Abbess of an English Benedictine Abbey in Rome, with permission from the Church and the Benedictines, opened the grave in Saint Luke Chapel. Her book, a life of Elena Piscopia, is listed in the *Bibliography* (see p 73). Abbess Pynsent credits as source information for her book the writings of Italian authors whose work she found in the Museo Civica at Padua. She also obtained records from the University of Padua of the famous graduation of 1678 and other records pertaining to Elena Piscopia and her family. She saw the statue

Apse, Saint Luke Chapel, with three gravesites. (Right, closeup) the open grave of Elena Cornaro Piscopia, awaiting restoration.

Foto Lufin Albano Terme (PD)

of Elena Piscopia in the University of Padua which had been the top of the sarcophagus erected by John Baptist in the Church of Saint Anthony.

The Abbess writes of replacing the Monks' original black marble marker, which had been cracked sometime after the Monks had reverently sealed the cypress coffin, two centuries ago. Regretably, the Abbess's replacement marker was fragmented during restoration work, since World War II. The Abbess also carefully replaced a leaden plate which she found inside the coffin. Translated it reads:

"Here rests Lucrezia Cornaro Piscopia, a Venetian Noble Woman of Famous Name, Virgin, Dedicated to God and Saint Benedict. Most Skilled in the Ancient Classical Languages of Hebrew, Latin, and Greek, Plus the Modern Languages of Spanish, French, and Italian, Which She Spoke Flawlessly and Fluently. Excelling in All Sciences, Publicly Granted a Doctoral Laureate at Padua, In the Year 1678, on the 26 Day of June, and Declared a Doctrix in the Catholic Church. Moved by Her Fame and Writings the Supreme Pontiff, Innocent XI, With the Apostolic Letters of May 6, and John III, King of Poland, With the Royal Letters of June 14, Visited Her. Also the Roman Emperor, Leopold I, and Charles III, Duke of Lotharinga, Highly Commended Her; Likewise Louis XIV, King of France, and Other Princes Bestowed Upon Her the Highest Honors. However, in the Same Year 1684, on the 26 Day of July, at 18 Hour, She Commuted This Mortal Glory for an Immortal One, to Receive the Double Aureole of Virgin and Doctor . . . in the 38 Year of Her Age. Her Surviving Parent, John Baptist (Procurator) of San Marco, Mourns Her Most Sorrowfully."

[In a letter following her visit to the Cornaro grave, Abbess Pynsent tells of placing on the tomb a large wreath of laurel and lillies "mingled with oak leaves and acorns." "All present," she says, "wrote their names on the lid of the new coffin and the date was added—we have kept the pen."]

(Background) Saint Justina, Renaissance Benedictine Abbey Church, replacing in 16th century a Romanesque-Gothic basilica. Adjoining the basilica, visible only in the rear, is Saint Luke Chapel—added in 1301 where in the mortuary at her request Elena Cornaro Piscopia was buried among the Benedictine monks. *(Profile p 41)*

(Foreground) Beautiful Prato della Valle, Padua

Foto Lufin Albano Terme (PD)

Marble bust of Elena Cornaro Piscopia placed in the Church of
Saint Anthony by her younger brother Jerome in a niche
above the site of a huge sarcophagus which her father had
commissioned to receive her body. (The sarcophagus was
never occupied—dismantled in 1727). (*Profile* p 42)

Museo Civico Padova

Eight names were signed on the lid: Mechtildis Pynsent Abb. OSB; M. Maurus Watson post. OSB; Jacobus A. Campbell, Rettor del Collegio Scozzese, Roma; Carlo Ferraris, Rettor della R. Universita; D. Marino Frattin OSB; S. Georgii Majoris Venetarum, Supr.; D. Domenico Puller, Parroco; Gaetano D. Varda, pel Municipio; Pel Cancilliare Vescovile Soc. Giovanni Campeis, Deleg. Speciale.

Thus, attesting to the content of the grave, and signing along with the Abbess Pynsent, were Rectors of two college faculties from Rome (Scottish and Italian) and dignitaries representing the Church in Venice and the City of Venice, and a special delegate representing the highest office of the State.

10. The Tercentenary Committees, Italy and the United States

COMITATO PER LE CELEBRAZIONI CENTENARIE DI ELENA LUCREZIA CORNARO PISCOPIA PRIMA DONNA LAUREATA NEL MONDO 1678.

Copresidenti: Prof. Aldo Stella per l'Università di Padova
P. Abate D. Innocenzo Negrato per l'Abbazia di S. Giustina

Secretaria Generale: Dr. Maria Tonzig
The United States Committee For Elena Lucrezia Cornaro Piscopia Tercentenary 1678-1978.

HONORARY CHAIRMEN

Dr. Sylvia E. Bowman, Chancellor of Regional Campuses
Indiana University
Rt. Rev. Egbert H. Donovan, O.S.B. Archabbot
St. Vincent Archabbey

Dr. Charles J. Hitch, President
  University of California, Berkeley
Mr. Alfred M. Hunt, Trustee
  The Hunt Foundation of Pittsburgh
Dr. Wesley W. Posvar, Chancellor
  University of Pittsburgh
Rt. Rev. Benedict Reid, O.S.B., Abbot
  St. Gregory's Abbey
Dr. Alan Simpson, President
  Vassar College
Dr. David B. Truman, President
  Mt. Holyoke College

SPONSORING ORGANIZATIONS

International

International Federation of University Women

National

American Association of University Women
National Council of Catholic Women
Kappa Gamma Pi, National Catholic College Women's
  Honor Society
Women's Alumnae Club Council of Pittsburgh
  (Ad Hoc National Committee)
National Council of Administrative Women in Education

EXECUTIVE COMMITTEE

Officers

Mrs. Ruth Crawford Mitchell, Chairman
Mrs. E. Maxine Bruhns, Vice-Chairman
Mrs. Beatrice Gullion, Recording Secretary
Mrs. George F. Alderdice, Jr., Treasurer

[110]

Committee Chairmen
   Mrs. C. V. Starrett, Editorial
   Mrs. William F. Haushalter, Library
   Mrs. William H. Guernsey, Promotion
   Mrs. Wilfred J. Finegold, Distribution
   Dr. Francesca Colecchia, Translation
   Miss Savina Skewis, Hospitality

Members
   Mrs. John C. Bongiovanni, National Council of
      Catholic Women
   Mrs. George Coraluppi, Padua Committee Representative
   Mrs. Arthur R. Forbush, Washington, D.C. Representative
   Mrs. Cyril A. Fox, Jr., Women's Alumnae Club Council
   Mrs. Justin R. Noetzel, Kappa Gamma Pi
   Mrs. Derrick A. Sherman, American Association of
      University Women
   Mrs. William H. Woodwell, Vassar Club of Pittsburgh

GENERAL COMMITTEE—PITTSBURGH
   Administrative Women in Education
   Amita
   Carlow College
   Carnegie-Mellon University
   Carnegie Library
   Chatham College
   College Club
   Council of Catholic Women
   Dante Alighieri Society
   Duquesne University
   Italian Room Committee, Cathedral of Learning
   Seton Hill College
   University of Pittsburgh
   Vassar College—Class of 1912
   Women's Alumnae Club Council
   Young Women's Christian Association

II.   Editor's Acknowledgements

To name all who with material aid or with encouragement
have helped the Editor is impossible. The list is very long.
Some should be named in any note of acknowledgement,
however brief, although description of their help falls short
of its reality. My gratitude is deep and sincere—for those men-
tioned and for many others.

Especially, I thank two friends: (1) Mr. Alfred M. Hunt, for
choosing me to edit and coordinate the individually authored
divisions of the Book, for wanting me to write this Glossary
explaining much that falls within a *Profile of Elena Piscopia,* but
outside the purview of the authors of the Book's individual
divisions, and for asking me to work in the physical designing
of the Book with the master printer and typographer Mr.
Thomas Pears, III. (2) Dr. Ruth Crawford Mitchell, for helpful
criticism and extraordinary patience and drive. Her unflagging
devotion to the Paduan scholar whose life gives life to the
Book; her rare skill in gathering from both sides of the Atlantic
men and women with a variety of talents needed to push
forward the Book and to place it ultimately in resource

libraries around the world—these, her strengths, have been the greatest bulwark for all who have contributed imagination and energy to the complications of the work. Her *Introduction* stands tribute to her creative gifts.

No words can thank adequately the whole-souled Paduan Dr. Maria Tonzig or pay tribute worthy her contribution. Her kindness, matching her scholarship, shortened distance and surmounted language barriers. Among her distinctions is one which gives her a unique place in the story of the Benedictine Oblate and Scholar, Elena *Scholastica* Cornaro Piscopia. Dr. Tonzig, in 1925, was first to be made a Benedictine Oblate after the Order was expelled from Italy by Napoleonic decree more than a century before, and after the Monks and Abbots were permitted to return in 1919. Not more highly prized by her is the doctorate she was awarded in 1925 for scholarship in philosophy and for her thesis, a history of the church of Saint Justina. Her definitive Bibliography printed in this Book stands tribute to her scholarship.

I thank also, Mr. John Halmaghi, Bibliographer of the Hillman Library, University of Pittsburgh, for his professional help, and I thank Miss Hazel Johnson and Mrs. Glenora Rossell, those remarkable Hillman librarians!

High among those to be thanked, professionally, is the local artist, the late Norton Peterson, whose talent adds the beauty of baroque design to title page, division titles, and chapter heads. His friendship will be cherished always.

Highly rated, also, are those whose translations of Italian and Latin documents, books, letters, and inscriptions on gravemarkers and statues have been very helpful: Professor Francesca Colecchia, Duquesne University; Classics Professor Emeritus Arthur Young, University of Pittsburgh; Mr. Frank Pleasant, Hillman Library; Mr. and Mrs. George Coraluppi and their business associate Mrs. Gina Broderick; and the Benedictine scholars of the Archabbey at Latrobe, Pennsylvania—Father Ildephonse and Father Finton Shoniker, Librarian of the Saint Vincent College and of the Archabbey.

Committee lists in this Glossary are a litany of names of those whose unselfish service has been truly "a labor of love." They have a very real place in this book, and I am proud to be listed with them.

I should be remiss indeed if I failed to include thanks to Mrs. Fred Bruhns (Maxine), Director of the University of Pittsburgh's Nationality & International Exchange Programs, her assistants Mrs. Maxine Walker and Miss Catherine Ekimoff, Mrs. Arthur Agras (Artemis), Secretary to Mrs. Mitchell, and my Bradford School student typists, Miss Karen Gilbert and Miss Ellen Kriss.

Dr. Albert C. Van Dusen, Vice Chancellor and Secretary of the University of Pittsburgh, has been a good friend to me and to the Book—as always, confidence and help beyond measuring.

Dr. Ruth Crawford Mitchell adds here a list of her acknowledgements. There are so many to whom both of us are grateful.

We thank Mrs. Gabrielle Forbush, who has used her graceful pen, diligently and professionally, for articles about Elena Cornaro Piscopia in periodicals and other publications. Especially, Mrs. Mitchell thanks the Class of 1912, Vassar College, especially, Mrs. Earle M. Craig and Miss Florence O. Wilson, for constant and generous support.

The entire Committee is grateful to the Abbot Primate of the venerable Order of Benedictines, Father Rembert G. Weakland—*a Pittsburgher*. He bridged for us two cultural worlds, and his sound judgment and sensitive understanding brought to fruition our plans for helping with this volume to restore the grave of Elena Lucrezia *Scholastica* Cornaro Piscopia, the *Prima Donna Laureata nel Mondo*.

AGNES L. STARRETT

[114]

COLOPHON

A First Edition of this book has been printed for The United States Committee for the Elena Lucrezia Cornaro Piscopia Tercentenary, Pittsburgh, Pennsylvania, U.S.A.

It was set by Davis & Warde, Inc., Pittsburgh, Pennsylvania, in Hunt Roman type designed by Hermann Zapf and Monotype Spectrum designed by J. Van Krimpen. It is printed on Curtis Rag Paper by the Meriden Gravure Company, Meriden, Connecticut, and bound in Columbia Riverside Linen cloth Venetian Red by Tapley-Rutter Company, Inc., Moonachie, New Jersey. The book was designed by Thomas C. Pears III and Agnes L. Starrett, Pittsburgh, Pennsylvania.